Call No One on Earth Your Father

Call No One on Earth Your Father

*Revisioning the Ordained Ministry
in the Contemporary Catholic Church*

JOSEPHINE E. ARMOUR

WIPF & STOCK · Eugene, Oregon

CALL NO ONE ON EARTH YOUR FATHER
Revisioning the Ordained Ministry in the Contemporary Catholic Church

Copyright © 2019 Josephine E. Armour. All rights reserved. Except for brief quotations in critical publications or reviews, no part of this book may be reproduced in any manner without prior written permission from the publisher. Write: Permissions, Wipf and Stock Publishers, 199 W. 8th Ave., Suite 3, Eugene, OR 97401.

Wipf & Stock
An Imprint of Wipf and Stock Publishers
199 W. 8th Ave., Suite 3
Eugene, OR 97401

www.wipfandstock.com

PAPERBACK ISBN: 978-1-5326-7424-2
HARDCOVER ISBN: 978-1-5326-7425-9
EBOOK ISBN: 978-1-5326-7426-6

Manufactured in the U.S.A.   MARCH 18, 2019

In Memory

Monsignor Denis Edwards

Theologian and priest of great integrity

10th December, 1943–5th March, 2019

Contents

Acknowledgements | ix

Introduction | xi

Part One A Critique of the Traditional Theology of the Ordained Ministry | 1

    1 The Ordained Ministry: "Set Apart for the Church" | 3

    2 Who Selects the Ministers of the Church? | 11

    3 The Hierarchical Ordering and Elevation of the Ordained Ministry | 15

    4 "Marked with a Special Character" | 25

    5 The Symbolic Role of the Priesthood | 30

    6 The Mystification of the Eucharist | 38

    7 The Requirement of Celibacy for Ordained Ministry | 44

    8 The Exclusion of Women from the Ordained Ministry | 50

Part Two Retrieving Relevant Understandings from the Tradition | 57

    9 Retrieving the Egalitarian Nature of the Early Christian Movement | 59

    10 Retrieving the Significance of Baptism for Ministry | 63

    11 Retrieving the Story of Women's Leadership in the Early Christian Movement | 68

    12 Retrieving the Prophetic Voices of Women | 72

    13 Retrieving the Notion of *Diakonia* | 79

    14 Retrieving the Doctrine of the Trinity | 84

Part Three   Revisioning the Ordained Ministry | 93

    15   The Symbol of the Trinity | 95

    16   Ordained Ministry: An Expression of the God who is Three Persons in Mutual Relationship | 100

    17   Ordained Ministry: Manifesting the Mutual and Nonhierarchical Nature of God | 107

    18   Ordained Ministry: A Focus of the Unity and Diversity of God | 116

    19   Ordained Ministry: Manifesting the Ecstasy of God | 120

    20   The Need for the Democratization of the Church | 123

    21   Conclusion | 131

Bibliography | 135

Acknowledgements

THIS BOOK HAS SAT on the shelf unpublished for some years! It is drawn from the research of my doctoral thesis written in 2000.

In the late 1980s I left the Anglican Church where I was studying theology as an ordination candidate in a diocese that had not yet voted in favor of women's ordination. Attracted by the vigorous discussions of feminist theologians amongst the Dominican sisterhood, I became a Catholic and joined the Dominican Sisters of Holy Cross Congregation in Adelaide, South Australia.

It is to them that I owe much gratitude as they gave me the encouragement and opportunities to continue studying and to write. I remember with love Margaret Cain, OP and Susan Sullivan, OP, who both left this life too early and were such strong mentors for me. I also thank Angela Moloney, OP, for her courage and integrity, Bernadette Kiley, OP, for her fine scholarship and expertise as a teacher, and Maureen O'Connell, OP, Patricia Brady OP and Ann Burr, OP, who have never ceased to offer their encouragement and inspiration.

For myself, I have always felt a call to the ordained ministry. That never left me, despite my reception into a church that did not look likely to change on this issue for some time. For twenty-five years, I hoped that things would change, but they have not. In 2017, I made a momentous decision to return to the Anglican Church where I now prepare for ministry as a provisional ordinand.

This book strongly critiques the traditional theology of the ordained ministry in the Roman Catholic Church. Nevertheless, I acknowledge those ordained men who have been an inspiration to me. Thank you to Denis Edwards, Michael Trainor, and Tony Densley.

Thank you to Sheila Flynn, OP and Bill Goodes, who read this document from beginning to end and offered such helpful comments and corrections.

Thank you to Jill for the precious gift of friendship.

Introduction

THERE EXISTS A CRISIS in the ministry of the Roman Catholic Church, some signs of which are immediately observable. The most glaring current sign of brokenness has been the exposure of significant clergy involvement in the sexual abuse of children and in the suppression of information about these scandals by responsible officeholders of the church. Many Catholics have become disillusioned as they have seen once trusted clerics put on trial in the civil courts. How did this scandalous state amongst the ordained ministry arise?

An elderly priest once confided in me, "As a young priest I was the apple of my mother's eye. I was respected and admired by all of my family and friends, but today the priesthood has become a millstone around my neck." Today, perhaps it is not surprising that far fewer men present themselves to the church to be considered for the ordained ministry. Coupled with this fact is the situation—in Australia at least—of a growing number of Roman Catholic communities that are unable to fully participate in the sacraments of the church because there is no ordained priest available. People in many regions of Australia, both in the suburbs and in rural Australia, have less access to the celebration of the Eucharist, and in more remote regions of the country there is sometimes no ordained priest to anoint the sick and dying, or to provide the sacrament of reconciliation. This phenomenon is occurring in a church that has highly valued its sacramental tradition over the centuries and for which the Eucharist is the principal form of worship. There is no doubting the fact that the ordained ministry of the contemporary Roman Catholic Church is in crisis and that the task of building up the Christian community is hindered by this crisis.

The scope of this book is not to demonstrate this fact. That there is a crisis in the ministry of the Roman Catholic Church is assumed. That crisis is patently obvious not only within the Church but to the wider community.

Introduction

What this book sets out to do is to critique the traditional theology and practice of the ordained ministry and present a renewed theology that can address this crisis.

The theology of the ordained ministry is not static, but has developed over the centuries as the church has become institutionalized. It is a theology which has fostered clericalism: that is, it has valued a hierarchical form of order and has attributed an elevated status to the ordained ministry. It has not placed the ordained ministry in its rightful context within the Christian community, but has rather tended to view the ordained as "set apart" for a particular work over against the rest of the laity. The notion of the ontological and indelible character of the ordained, the notion of the sacred power of the ordained, priestly representation, and the notion of the ordained minister as "servant" are discussed in the following pages.

This book brings a critique to current practices in the Roman Catholic Church, including the lifelong commitment to the ordained ministry, the requirement of celibacy amongst the ordained ministry and the exclusion of women from the ordained ministry. It will take up the task of historical retrieval, reviewing the tradition in order to reclaim or recover elements that may have been distorted, lost, or forgotten. It asks, "What is retrievable in the tradition that is freeing and redeeming for a renewed theology?"

The critique of the traditional theology and current practices in the ordained ministry and the retrieval of relevant elements of the tradition are a springboard for reconstructing a theology of the ordained ministry. Inspired by Catherine LaCugna's[1] suggestion that the Trinity can act as a basis for ecclesial life, I suggest that the triune God can be an image for the ordained ministry itself and, through its relational nature, the ministry of the whole church. The doctrine of the Trinity is a basis for setting the ordained ministry into its rightful context of the Christian community where all of the gifts of the baptized are valued and where ministry is collaborative, non-hierarchical, and mutually enriching for all of God's people.

The ordained ministry is a particular ministry within the broader mission and ministry of the church. I use the wider term, ministry, to refer to the public activity of a baptized follower of Jesus Christ that is carried out on behalf of the Christian community for the purposes of building up and nourishing the people of God. Ministry cannot be carried out in isolation: it must be conducted in relation to others. As John Zizioulas has pointed

---

1. LaCugna, *God for Us*, 400–3.

Introduction

out, "without the notion of 'relationship' the ministry loses its character both as a charisma of the Spirit . . . and as service."[2]

The term "ministry" is to be distinguished from both Christian discipleship and the mission of the church to which all baptized Christians are called. Although it is the responsibility of all baptized Christians to ensure that the ministry of the church is ongoing, it is not necessarily the charge of all Christians to carry out that ministry. The public work of ministry ought to be carried out by those with the gifts, skills, and vocation to do so. Whether one has the necessary gifts, skills, and vocation to be a minister is a question that ought to be discerned within the Christian community. Furthermore, the discernment of suitability for the ordained ministry in particular, ought to take place at a local level but with the sanction or ratification of the universal church.

Edward Schillebeeckx, one of the most respected theologians of the last century, opened his expanded work on ministry, *The Church with a Human Face,* by lamenting the crisis facing the ordained ministry of the church. He writes:

> The dominant conceptions about the practice and the theology of the ministry seem to be robbing the gospel of its force in communities of believers—an experience that is shared by quite a number of Christians and ministers.[3]

Schillebeeckx's claim is a serious one, since the gospel message ought to be that which brings hope to the Christian community. Susan Ross, some twenty-five years ago, made her evaluation of the church in terms of this very quality. She argued, "[t]he extent to which structures and institutions serve the message of the gospel is the measure of their value."[4] In the light of such comments, I seek to bring the contemporary form, structure, practice, and theology of the ordained ministry in the Roman Catholic Church under scrutiny.

I introduce Edward Schillebeeckx as a partner in this theological dialogue, because he has been open to the experiences of women in the Roman Catholic Church and to reflecting upon their discontent. More than twenty years ago, he proclaimed the need for church leaders to heed the voice of women:

---

2. Zizioulas, *Being as Communion,* 220.
3. Schillebeeckx, *Church with a Human Face,* 1.
4. Ross, "God's Embodiment and Women," 203.

Introduction

> This discontent of women is no longer just a complaint; it has become a sharp accusation. As long as women in the church are completely excluded from all the authorities that make decisions, there can be no question of the true liberation of women in and through the church. Perhaps the criticism expressed by women (more than half of the church community) is at present the most fundamental charge leveled at the churches, and one that they cannot avoid. Such a massive, and now overwhelming, call for liberation which cannot be stifled, from the other half of the whole church, can no longer be held back; in the long run it will change the face of the church, and its structures of ministry as well.[5]

I write as a Christian feminist theologian in a field where there are many views that pertain to the ordained ministry of the church, ranging from the more conservative position,[6] which seeks justice by simply asking that women who feel called to the ordained ministry be able to test that vocation, to the more radical view that would hold that the Roman Catholic Church is so utterly patriarchal that there is little hope of altering present hierarchical structures. I propose a position that lies somewhere between these two: a position that seeks more than the mere incorporation of women into the present structure of the church's ministry, but a position conservative enough to believe that transformation of church structures is possible.

Feminist theologies frequently have their starting point in reflection upon women's experience of oppression. In her discussion of feminist theological method, Anne Carr described a threefold task entailing "a critique of the tradition, historical retrieval, and theological construction."[7] Each of these three tasks will form a framework for the dialogue presented in the following pages between a feminist perspective on ministry and Schillebeeckx's insights on ministry.

Feminist theologies of ministry have their roots in the articulated experience of women who encounter oppression within the structures, customs, and life of both church and society. A critique of the tradition entails asking pertinent questions about the silence, absence, or exclusion of

---

5. Schillebeeckx, *Church with a Human Face*, 239–40.

6. In early discussions amongst liberal feminists about women, ministry and church leadership often fell into this category of seeking justice for women by arguing for their inclusion into the full ministry of the church. However, the mere inclusion of women into a structure which is inherently patriarchal does not go far enough to bring the necessary changes. Feminists are radically critiquing the centralised hierarchalised structure and particular patriarchal theological notions which are employed to support that structure.

7. Carr and Fiorenza, *New Vision*, 11.

Introduction

women from the work of theology and in this case, more particularly, from the decision-making procedures and authorized ministry of the church. I critique the androcentric bias that has pervaded the tradition and the fact that down through the centuries women have been discouraged from being subjects of theological reflection. I challenge practices that ignore women's experience, or that deny or distort the full humanity of women. Rosemary Radford Ruether articulates a key principle underpinning a great deal of feminist theology:

> The critical principle of feminist theology is the promotion of the full humanity of women. Whatever denies, diminishes, or distorts the full humanity of women is therefore appraised as not redemptive. Theologically speaking, whatever diminishes or denies the full humanity of women must be presumed not to reflect the divine or an authentic relation to the divine, or to reflect the authentic nature of things, or to be the message or work of an authentic redeemer or a community of redemption.[8]

Ruether's requirement that the full humanity of women be honored has become something of a benchmark for feminist theologians. She has clearly articulated a basic expectation that full personhood must always be sought. In the light of this expectation, a critique of the practices and theologies of the Christian tradition is central to feminist theology.

The further task of historical retrieval involves the reviewing of the tradition, in order to reclaim or recover elements that may have been distorted, lost, or forgotten. A feminist approach asks, "What is retrievable in the tradition that is freeing and redeeming for women?" The task of this book will be not only to point to moments in the tradition when customs and practices came into being which were not redeeming for women, but also to attempt to retrieve those practices and occurrences in the tradition that do support the full humanity of women. Elisabeth Schüssler Fiorenza, in her analyses of early Christian women's experiences, raises these questions: "How can early Christian origins be reconstructed in such a way as to be understood as 'women's affairs'? In other words, is early Christian history 'our own' history or heritage? Were women as well as men the initiators of the Christian movement?"[9]

My hope is that this writing will be a contribution to current work in ecclesiology by challenging current ecclesial practices in the Roman

---

8. Ruether, *Sexism and God-talk*, 18–19.
9. Fiorenza, *In Memory of Her*, xviii.

Introduction

Catholic Church and suggesting new ways of viewing the ordained ministry. This view is consistent with Edward Schillebeeckx's claim that changes in the practice of the ministry are not only "quite legitimate in the light of the gospel," but also "necessary for the vitality of the gospel in Christian communities at the present time."[10] Schillebeeckx lamented the failure of the institutional church to create structural change in order to integrate the new elements that arose from the Second Vatican Council:

> And when [the] Christian freedom recognized by the Council was not subsequently guaranteed and protected by church law, this promise became an empty gesture, without any evangelical influence on our history. Then the breath of the Council was cut off and its spirit, the Holy Spirit, was extinguished. Then, by virtue of various concerns (which were often matters of church politics), church hierarchies achieved an uncontrolled power over men and women of God, "God's people on the way," who had been put under tutelage.[11]

---

10. Schillebeeckx, *Church with a Human Face*, 2.
11. Schillebeeckx, *Church with a Human Face*, xiv.

PART ONE

A Critique of the Traditional Theology of the Ordained Ministry

THE FOLLOWING CHAPTERS CRITIQUE the setting apart of the ordained ministry from the Christian community that resulted in division between the clergy and the laity.[1] I critique the hierarchical ordering and elevated status of the ministerial offices of the church, and the lack of lay involvement in the selection of ministers. Notions of the ontological character and of the sacred power of the minister will be challenged, along with the representative role of the ordained minister. Clericalism within the ministry, I will suggest, has been consolidated historically by the mystification of the Eucharist over the centuries. Finally, I question the exclusion of women, the requirement of celibacy, and the need for a lifelong commitment to the ordained ministry.

---

1. I use the term "laity" as it is commonly used, i.e., to refer to those not ordained, although the term originally referred to the whole of the people of God: the *laos*.

1

The Ordained Ministry: "Set Apart for the Church"

Traditional theology in the Roman Catholic Church has viewed the ordained as set apart for a particular work over against the rest of the laity. The *Catechism of the Catholic Church* explains that "ordination is also called *consecratio*, for it is a setting apart and an investiture by Christ himself for his church."[1] The *Catechism*, although acknowledging that both the ministerial priesthood and the common priesthood participate in the one priesthood of Christ, seeks carefully to show that these two differ in essence:

> The ministerial or hierarchical priesthood of bishops and priests, and the common priesthood of all the faithful participate, "each in its own proper way, in the one priesthood of Christ." While being "ordered to one another," they differ essentially. In what sense? While the common priesthood of the faithful is exercised by the unfolding of baptismal grace a life of faith, hope and charity, a life according to the Spirit the ministerial priesthood is at the service of the common priesthood. It is directed at the unfolding of the baptismal grace of all Christians.[2]

The fact that the ministerial priesthood is to be at the service of the common priesthood in order to build up the Christian community is used in the *Catechism* to show how it differs in essence from the common priesthood.

---

1. *Catechism of the Catholic Church*, 1538.
2. *Catechism of the Catholic Church*, 1547.

Part One—A Critique of the Traditional Theology

The documents of the Second Vatican Council also affirm a difference in essence. "Though they differ from one another in essence and not only in degree, the common priesthood of the faithful and the ministerial or hierarchical priesthood are nonetheless interrelated."[3]

I propose that it is preferable to emphasize not the point of difference between the common priesthood and the ministerial priesthood, but the point of relatedness. Being "at the service of the common priesthood" describes how the ministerial priesthood is *related* to the common priesthood.

Ordained ministers are rightly *appointed within and for* the community, but not, I suggest, *set apart from* the community. Historically it can be demonstrated that the ordained ministry has not only been set apart from the community which it serves, but separated from this context.

Edward Schillebeeckx has demonstrated this historical separation of the ordained ministry from the Christian community. He traces the historical development of the clergy/lay division that becomes apparent in the early Christian church in the gradual appropriation of various ministerial works by official church leadership. He notes that "[t]he earlier authorities in prophecy and teaching are now swallowed up and incorporated into the authority of the one local bishop."[4] He suggests that as early as the second century, the local leadership of the church had appropriated the roles of both prophets and teachers.[5] Once authority for ministry was lodged with the official church leadership, a trend towards clericalism began. This became pronounced at the time of Constantine and Theodosius, when Christianity was sanctioned throughout the empire as a state religion:

> The clergy began to encourage the attitude of hierarchical behavior in authority . . . The senior clergy in particular began gradually to take over the insignia of the emperor and of princes (they often came from noble families). In this way the church became clericalized, a development which from the perspective of the New Testament is clearly one against which the gospel warns. Believers (who from then on began to be called 'laity') ceased to be the subjects of faith, in the Spirit, and were reduced to being the objects of priestly care.[6]

---

3. Abbott, *Documents of Vatican II*, 27.
4. Schillebeeckx, *Church with a Human Face*, 71.
5. Schillebeeckx, *Church with a Human Face*, 85.
6. Schillebeeckx, *Church with a Human Face*, 204–5.

The separation of the ordained ministry from the Christian community, in conjunction with the hierarchical ordering of the ministry, has acted to disempower the baptized people of God and to foster clericalism. When the role of the ordained ministry is understood out of the context of and apart from the Christian community, a false division between the ordained and the rest of the baptized is created. That is not to say there is no distinction between the two. Although I argue that there is a distinctive role for the ordained ministry, false divisions have been constructed between clergy and laity that have served to hinder the work of Christian ministry. This has occurred when certain roles which are common to the vocation of all the baptized (i.e., to the common priesthood) are incorrectly attributed to the ministerial priesthood alone.

One of the insights of feminist theology is its challenge to language that emphasizes division and separation at the expense of connection and interrelationship. I have already mentioned a tendency in the Roman Catholic tradition to focus upon the differences between the ministerial priesthood and the common priesthood rather than the relationship between the two. At this point in time it is helpful to refrain from the search for the essential difference between the ministerial and common priesthood of all the baptized and to become more tolerant of the ambiguity that has arisen between these roles in the post-Vatican II church. Susan Ross argues that a sacramental theology ought to be open to and appreciative of ambiguity. Rigidity and legalism can not only diminish a sense of the sacred, "but pastoral opportunities for reaching those hungry for healing, nurture, reconciliation, and union are also endangered."[7]

Rebecca Chopp has noted that feminist theology moves away from oppositional thinking and recognizes richness and value in difference. One of the fundamental principles of feminism, Chopp argues, is that of "seeing and valuing through connection rather than opposition."[8] This is based on a fundamental belief in the relatedness of God and the world. She refers to thinking in philosophy, social science, and theology that identifies oppositional thinking as "one of the dominant and problematic patterns of the time."[9] There are dangers in interpreting information in dualities, and in relating differences in terms of opposition:

---

7. Ross, *Extravagant Affections*, 55.
8. Chopp, "In the Real World," 17.
9. Chopp, "In the Real World," 17.

Part One—A Critique of the Traditional Theology

> Feminist theologians offer a set of very different orientative principles based on a rich symbolism of relatedness of God and world. Feminist theologians see and value all the differences among people, and how these differences can relate in a variety of ways. Rather than oppositional thinking, feminist theology provides a kind of connected thinking that seeks to empathetically find positions of similarity and difference, and to see both as abundant riches.[10]

Mary Aquin O'Neill also comments upon the characteristic of feminist writing to bring together notions that have traditionally been cast as either/or. She observes that feminist writers are challenging dualistic thinking. "Women theologians are trying to hold together what had been cast as either/or, and to think out a theology based on interrelationships."[11]

Clare Watkins's work is an example of this mode of doing theology. Watkins comments upon formation for ministry in the United States:

> The way in which formation for ordination is carried out in this country tends to accentuate *difference* rather than similarity ... The separateness of training and formation adds weight to the sense that ordination sets a person apart from (rather than for) a community. Ordination represents, among other things, *a difference in the way of authorization*, ... This difference emphasizes acutely and, I suggest, unnecessarily, the difference between lay and ordained ministries both symbolically and practically.[12]

A renewed theology of the ordained ministry must seek to describe how the ministerial priesthood is related to the common priesthood. Oppositional thinking—which emphasizes the distinctiveness of the ministerial priesthood over and against the common priesthood—acts to create a false division between the two.

Distinctions between teachers and learners and between servants and those being served are specific examples of false and simplistic divisions that require challenge. Many in the Christian community are involved in both serving and being served, in teaching and being taught, and in ministering and receiving ministrations. In her critique of the division of the Roman Catholic Church community into teachers (clergy) and learners (the people), Mary Hines suggests that this is particularly problematic in

---

10. Chopp, "In the Real World," 17.
11. O'Neill, "Current Theology," 738.
12. Watkins, "Ministry, Muddle and Mystery," 88.

discussions concerning sexuality, where "the authoritative teachers are all celibate males."[13] To assume that the small group of the ordained has the wisdom in this matter and that the rest of the church ought to conform is highly problematic. I suggest that it is no coincidence that numerous cases of the sexual abuse of minors have occurred within a church that has maintained an exclusively male priesthood.

Leonardo Boff noted the dehumanizing effect of the rigid separation between clergy and laity: "The distinction between one Church that speaks and teaches and another that listens and obeys, and the claim of a clerical body to be the guardians of truth, has led to violence and the practice of a domination by some Christians over others."[14]

Boff demonstrated the diminution that is brought upon both the ministerial priesthood and the baptized people when a false division between teachers and learners is insisted upon. The work of listening and learning is properly the vocation of all baptized Christians, including the ordained. Those not ordained must confidently trust that their experience and point of view is worthy of others' hearing and has the potential to be a resource in the decision-making work of the church:

> On one side is the *Ecclesia docens* (the teaching church), which knows everything and interprets everything; on the other the laity who knows nothing, produce nothing and receive everything, the *Ecclesia discens*, (the learning church). The hierarchy learns nothing from contact with these lay people; they in their turn have no ecclesial space in which to demonstrate their riches. This denies the ontological vocation of every human being and every Christian in particular, which is to be a participant in and not merely a spectator of the history of salvation.[15]

This particular model of the *Ecclesia docens*, which Boff described, is a patriarchal model in which dominant males have power and authority over women, children, and other disenfranchised males.

One of the dangers of interpreting the role of the clergy out of the context of and apart from the Christian community is that the role of the rest of the baptized community in the mission and ministry of the church can be undervalued and overlooked. In such a view of church, a clericalism is encouraged, in which the non-ordained people of the church are

---

13. Hines, "Community for Liberation," 169.
14. Boff, "Matters Requiring Clarification," 47.
15. Boff, "Matters Requiring Clarification," 51.

Part One—A Critique of the Traditional Theology

confined to the role of recipients of the works of the ordained. Even where the non-ordained *are* involved in particular ministries of the church, such as pastoral work or chaplaincy, that work is often undervalued. Maria Harris discusses the use of the term "lay ministry," which she argues distinguishes the ministry of those not ordained from the "real ministry" that belongs to the officials of the church. Implicit in the use of the phrases, "ministry" and "lay ministry" are two kinds of ministry: the "real" ministry and a secondary (and unfortunately, second-class) ministry.[16] Harris surmises that it would be wise for Catholics to avoid the distinction between "ministry" and "lay ministry." Nevertheless, Catherine LaCugna argues that despite the increasing involvement of women in the ministry of the Roman Catholic Church, their work is not sacramentally recognized and is in fact, a second-class ministry:

> Women cannot be consecrated bishops nor ordained priests nor ordained deacons . . . Women cannot (officially) preach the Gospel. Women cannot mediate the grace of the Eucharist. Women's ministry is considered to be secondary, a supplement to ordained priesthood, which remains the real ministry.[17]

LaCugna observes that the work of non-ordained ministers, such as that of women in religious orders, has often been described as an apostolate, rather than a ministry. In fact the recent *Instruction on Certain Questions Regarding the Collaboration of the Non-Ordained Faithful in the Sacred Ministry of Priest* has specifically deemed it "unlawful for the non-ordained to assume titles such a "pastor", "chaplain", "co-ordinator", "moderator", or other such similar titles which can confuse their role and that of the Pastor, who is always a Bishop or Priest."[18]

The ministry of the church is the responsibility of *all* the baptized. This is not to suggest that all of the baptized will be ministers, but that there is a responsibility born out of baptism to ensure the ongoing work of building up the Christian community. Each baptized person needs to be alert to the ministerial gifts that are in the community and open to the potential of their own ministerial gifts. This responsibility for ministry, belonging to all the baptized, involves a grasping of our common vocation as disciples. Discipleship will not necessarily involve functioning as a minister in the church, but it will involve a commitment to the way of Christ and to the

---

16. Harris, "Questioning Lay Ministry," 97–109.
17. LaCugna, "Catholic Women as Ministers," 4–15.
18. John Paul II, *Instruction on Certain Questions*, 8.

building up of the Christian community. It will involve recognition of one's own and others' gifts and using those gifts for the common good.

During the historical process of the institutionalization of the church, the ordained ministry has tended to assume the responsibility for a vocation that rightfully belongs to all Christians. Instead of understanding the work of ministry as a partnership between the ordained and the non-ordained and between women and men, the traditional view of ministry sees the ordained ministry as primarily responsible for the teaching, sacramental, and administrative work of the church. Ruether recognizes the danger in such a one-sided approach to ministry that has generated almost endemic passivity in Roman Catholic congregations: "The clergy monopolize teaching, sacramental action, and administration and turn the community into passive dependents who are to receive these services from the clergy but cannot participate in shaping and defining themselves."[19]

Hervé Legrand makes the disturbing claim that the very identity of the ordained ministry could be somewhat reliant upon the passivity of the rest of the laity:

> One can see that the identity of the clergy is dialectically related to the religious dispossession of the laity (the "clerics" inculcate in the "laity" the latter's lack of knowledge and know-how) and to the parallel affirmation by the clergy of its own proper election and of its own proper superiority.[20]

Gloria Durka has recognized that the danger of locating decision-making power and authority solely in the hands of the ordained ministry is a resulting disempowerment for the people of God. She laments the consequences of growing clericalism: "The development of the clergy-laity division over the centuries, together with the control of ministries by the hierarchy, has impoverished the Church and left the laity in a position of passivity and powerlessness."[21]

When it is only the ordained who are involved in a significant way in the decision-making procedures of the church, the enormous body of the baptized people of God is denied its rightful responsibility in contributing to the mission and ministry of the church. It needs to be acknowledged that in various locales particularly in Western Europe, the United States, and in Australia there are in fact, examples of lay involvement in decision-making

---

19. Ruether, *Women-Church*, 75.
20. LeGrand, "La Réalisation," 184.
21. Durka, "Is Partnership Possible?," 47.

about the mission and ministry of the local church. However, I argue that the beneficial effect of these examples is overshadowed by the centralized authority of the Roman curia that acts to curb and even obstruct the decisions which are made at a local level.

Miroslav Volf argues convincingly that when priority is assigned to the office-holders of the church, the contribution of the laity to the worship of the church is suppressed and the passivity of the people of God is the end result: "The ecclesiological obscuring of the lay role in constituting the church is one of the most important *theological* factors contributing to lay passivity."[22]

There is a disempowering effect that arises from a false division between the ordained and the baptized community, which not only affects the baptized people of the Christian community, but also has wider implications. Letty Russell draws attention to the power of clericalism to hinder the work of the church in the wider society: "A line between clergy and laity tends to perpetuate a hierarchical system which places severe limitations on the relevance of the church to modern society and the ability of the church to serve where it is needed in that society."[23]

The voices of feminist and liberation theologians that I have mentioned add weight to the argument that the ordained ministry ought not be interpreted as an entity outside or separate from the community. Rather, it is essential that the ordained ministry be viewed as fundamentally related to the Christian community. As Schillebeeckx has claimed, there is "no ministry without community."[24]

---

22. Volf, *After Our Likeness*, 227.
23. Russell, "Women and Ministry," 52.
24. Schillebeeckx, *Church with a Human Face*, 128.

2

Who Selects the Ministers of the Church?

ONE OF THE MANIFESTATIONS of the separation of the ordained ministry from the rest of the baptized community has been the exclusion of the community from the process of selecting ministers. The selection of ministers in the contemporary Roman Catholic Church is considered to be the responsibility of the bishops. The *Catechism of the Catholic Church* rightly acknowledges that the gift of ministry derives from Christ. "[I]t is Christ whose gift it is that some be apostles, others pastors."[1] Nevertheless the responsibility for the discernment of who are to be the pastors of the church is understood to rest with the bishops, as is the conferral of ordination: "Anyone who thinks he recognizes the signs of God's call to the ordained ministry must humbly submit his desire to the authority of the Church, who has the responsibility and right to call someone to receive orders."[2]

Whilst it seems a reasonable practice that those who discern a vocation to ministry ought to submit this to the authority of the church, this has come to mean the authority of the bishops. "It is for the bishops as the successors of the apostles to hand on the 'gift of the Spirit' . . . Validly ordained bishops, ie., those who are in the line of apostolic succession, validly confer the three degrees of the sacrament of Holy Orders."[3]

---

1. *Catechism of the Catholic Church*, 1575.
2. *Catechism of the Catholic Church*, 1578.
3. *Catechism of the Catholic Church*, 1576.

Part One—A Critique of the Traditional Theology

By means of his historical overview, Schillebeeckx critiques the inability of the Christian community to contribute to the choosing of their ministers, and makes a strong case for retrieving the ancient practice of involving the Christian community in the selection of its leadership. He observes that the leaders in the ancient church arose out of the community with the approbation and confirmation of the community. Empowered by their baptism in the Spirit, they worked to build up and nourish the Christian community. The leaders of these early Christian communities were at the service of and accountable to the people. Schillebeeckx recalls this history and critiques the change in which church leaders came to be appointed without the involvement of the Christian community and where men could now be ordained who have little or no connection with a particular community. For Schillebeeckx, there is no doubt that the ministry of the early Christians was "in no way detached from the community."[4] The Christian community was itself "the womb of the ministry."[5]

Feminist scholars critique the loss of the role of the community in choosing its ministers. Margaret Ulloa asks the question:

> Why should those communities not return to an earlier practice of the church and propose to the bishop for ordination those leaders who emerge naturally, or who feel called to offer this service to their own brothers and sisters? . . . The essential requirements in each community would be met by the gifts of that community, with responsibilities shared between a number of members, not asking of the one ordained to preside at the Eucharist that he or she be all things to all people.[6]

Rosemary Radford Ruether argues that the process of both selecting and educating the ordained ministry should arise from within the community: "The designating of a person as an ordained leader of a congregation should then be carried out in such a way as to show that it is the community itself which ordains her or him."[7] I maintain that it is both the community and the universal church that bestows ordination, not the community alone as Ruether suggests. However, ordination ought not to be bestowed entirely by the official church without the consultation of the local community. What must not go unheeded, as Ruether, Ulloa, and Schillebeeckx make

---

4. Schillebeeckx, *Church with a Human Face*, 83.
5. Schillebeeckx, *Church with a Human Face*, 207.
6. Ulloa, "Extending Ordained Ministry," 11.
7. Ruether, *New Woman, New Earth*, 81.

clear, is the role of the believing community in the choice of their ministers. Ruether rightly argues in a later article: "Leadership is called from within the community rather than imposed upon it from without in a way that deprives the community of its own self-articulation."[8]

Elisabeth Schüssler Fiorenza is a further voice critiquing the loss of the community's ability to choose their ministers. She attributes the restriction of community involvement to the reemergence of patriarchy. She notes that the shift from communal authority to the authority of office evolved over time to "absorb not only the teaching authority of the prophet and apostle but also the decision-making power of the community."[9] Furthermore, she argues, this shift to the authority of office meant that leadership was no longer accessible to all the baptized but was restricted to male heads of households.[10] The wider role of the Christian community in the choosing of its ministers became severely limited.

Schillebeeckx discusses the role of the Tridentine Council, which minimized the role of the believing community in the nomination of ordained ministers. He maintains that the Council of Trent "rightly had to combat the attempts of the nobility—at that time the laity were the ones who had the power—to nominate bishops and priests."[11] However it is important to note that not all of the laity were exercising the power to nominate ministers. It was the nobility who were abusing their economic and social privilege to nominate men to the ordained ministry who would further their interests and privileges. In fact, as historian Alexander Flick points out, by the close of the fifteenth century in Western Europe, "the nobles monopolized practically all of the most lucrative appointments in the State and the Church."[12] This situation suggests the extent of the process of patriarchalization in which privileged males came to wield such power in the Western church. The solution that the Tridentine Council proposed to counter the power of the nobles was that of ensuring that only the bishop would have the power to nominate and select other ordained ministers.[13] In this way, the Christian community as a whole is prevented from exercising what had earlier been their right to an involvement in the nomination and

8. Ruether, "Feminist Theology and Spirituality," 29.
9. Fiorenza, *In Memory of Her*, 286.
10. Fiorenza, *In Memory of Her*, 286–87.
11. Schillebeeckx, *Church with a Human Face*, 200.
12. Flick, *Decline*, 276.
13. Denzinger, *Enchiridion Symbolorum*, 414.

selection of ordained ministers. The choice of ministers moves from a noble elite to a clerical elite, from one form of patriarchal domination to another.

The vocation to ministry arises, and is perceived and made known within the local community. The church could indeed return to the earlier ecclesial understanding of ministry, as Ulloa and Schillebeeckx suggest, in which the role of the community in choosing its ministers could be restored. The justification for this restoration is not that it was the practice of the ancient church, but rather that there are good and just reasons for doing so. It is helpful to recall Sandra Schneider's warning that the church cannot simply imitate the practices of the early church without continual evaluation of those practices in the light of what is "good, true and just"[14] for the church today. That a practice belonged to the early church is not sufficient grounds for maintaining that practice in the twenty-first century. Rather, discerning whether a practice, teaching, or doctrine acts to assist in the work of building the Christian community and honoring the full humanity of all persons is a more suitable criterion for maintaining a practice or establishing a new practice.

---

14. .Schneiders, "Bible and Feminism," 45.

3

The Hierarchical Ordering and Elevation of the Ordained Ministry

EDWARD SCHILLEBEECKX AND MANY feminist thinkers have critiqued the hierarchical ordering and elevated status of the ordained ministry. The threefold ministry of the church ought not to be ordered in a hierarchical mode; that is, it ought not to be successively graded or ranked such that those higher in the hierarchy are understood to have power over those below. The ordained ministry ought not be understood as having a status more elevated than that of the rest of the baptized. Schillebeeckx questions the validity of the hierarchical form of the church's leadership and rightly suggests that it is not in fact in keeping with the message of the gospels:

> [A]ll the gospels are fiercely opposed to a hierarchical leadership 'in the way of the world'. Authority lies in love which serves the church, a service; it is not social, let alone ontological, status. This is really the essential feature of what the New Testament has to say about ministry and leadership in the church.[1]

By tracing the data of history, Schillebeeckx has demonstrated that the structure of the ministry of the church has not always been hierarchical in form. He argues that the early Christian movement resisted hierarchical organization and he draws attention to the admonition:

---

1. Schillebeeckx, *Church with a Human Face*, 204.

Part One—A Critique of the Traditional Theology

> And call no-one your father on earth, for you have one Father—the one in heaven. Nor are you to be called instructors, for you have one instructor, the Messiah. The greatest among you will be your servant. All who exalt themselves will be humbled, and all who humble themselves will be exalted. (Matt 23:9)[2]

Schillebeeckx argues that this is "fundamentally . . . the view of all the primitive Christian communities."[3] Schillebeeckx's demonstration of the fact that the church's ministry has not always been hierarchically ordered invites us to consider other possibilities for organizing ministry today.

A critique of hierarchical form has characterized the writing of many feminist thinkers. Schüssler Fiorenza, like Schillebeeckx, is struck by the irony of the Matthean text, "Call no-one your father on earth." She suggests that the early discipleship of equals would have rejected the patriarchal power of fathers and teachers and understood itself to have one father and teacher in God. She describes the early Christian movement: "[I]t is constituted and taught by one, and only one, teacher . . . The 'father' God is invoked here, however, not to justify patriarchal structures and relationships in the community of disciples but precisely to reject all such claims, powers, and structures."[4]

Schüssler Fiorenza draws attention to the fact that the church has not obeyed Jesus's command in this matter and has in fact legitimized ecclesial patriarchy, using the term "Father" for its ministers and thereby "using the name of God in vain."[5] As Schüssler Fiorenza claims, this saying of Jesus in fact uses the word Father for God, "not as a legitimization for existing patriarchal power structures in society or church but as a critical subversion of all structures of domination."[6] She asserts that the earliest Christian community was "egalitarian and not hierarchically ordered,"[7] understanding itself as a discipleship of equals. Rather, it has been the process of patriarchalization that has brought church structures to a hierarchalized form.

Elisabeth Schüssler Fiorenza describes the functioning of the hierarchy of the church in her systemic analysis of the "Constantinian Roman Kyriarchal Model of Church" which displays a pyramid locating "God: Father

2. Unless otherwise indicated, all biblical references are from NRSV.
3. Schillebeeckx, *Church with a Human Face*, 88.
4. Fiorenza, *In Memory of Her*, 150.
5. Fiorenza, *In Memory of Her*, 151.
6. Fiorenza, *In Memory of Her*, 151.
7. Fiorenza, *In Memory of Her*, 72.

and King" at the apex, the clergy in the upper half of the pyramid and the laity in the lower half.[8] The clergy are then ranked from the apex: the Holy Father, curia-cardinals, bishops, priests, and deacons. Even the laity in the lower half of the pyramid can be hierarchically ranked with celibates before non-celibates, the married before the divorced or homosexual, men before women, Catholic before Protestant and finally non-Christians at the base of the pyramid. Each level of the hierarchy has power over and is accorded status over levels below their own. Schillebeeckx sees a similar picture: "In the Neoplatonic-hierarchical conception of the church, the church forms a pyramid, a multi-stage system: God, Christ, the Pope, the bishops, priests and deacons; below these the religious and then the 'laity': first the men and finally the women and children."[9]

Although there is little discrepancy between Schüssler Fiorenza and Schillebeeckx in the description of the *outcome* of the process that gradually stifled the egalitarian strand within the early Christian movement, each describes the process differently. Once patriarchy became enshrined in the forms of ministry and in the structures of the church, the egalitarian strand once evident was hugely diminished. Elisabeth Schüssler Fiorenza demonstrates that it was as early as the second century that the church and its ministry became "patriarchalized."[10] She has coined the term, *kyriarchy*, to speak of the "rule of the emperor/master/lord/father/husband over his subordinates."[11] She indicates with this word, "that elite Western educated propertied Euro-American men have articulated and benefited from women's and other 'non-persons' exploitation."[12] Gerda Lerner has also alluded to this distinction in her description of patriarchy in her seminal work, *The Creation of Patriarchy*:

> *Patriarchy* in its wider definition means the manifestation and institutionalization of male dominance over women and children in the family and the extension of male dominance over women in society in general. It implies that men hold power in all the important institutions of society and that women are deprived of access to such power. It does *not* imply that women are either totally powerless or totally deprived of rights, influence and resources.[13]

8. Fiorenza, *unpublished notes*.
9. Schillebeeckx, *Church with a Human Face*, 198.
10. Fiorenza, *In Memory of Her*, 285–87.
11. Fiorenza, *Jesus*, 14.
12. Fiorenza, *Jesus*, 14.
13. Lerner, *Creation of Patriarchy*, 239.

Part One—A Critique of the Traditional Theology

Schüssler Fiorenza's clarification of the term patriarchy is a helpful one which furthers the discussion in a church where administrative and decision-making power at its highest level is confined to ordained males and from which not only women, but also all baptized and non-ordained people are excluded.

Schillebeeckx seems aware of this process of "patriarchalization," although he does not name it as such. Rather he speaks of the "institutionalization" of the church,[14] as "a certain tendency towards formalization" in the ministry of the church[15] and "the gradual centralization of ministry."[16] His description of the process in which the church "followed the civil trend in which the voice of the people was gradually stifled"[17] does not however highlight the fact that those who were in positions of leadership were, by this time, exclusively male. Schillebeeckx is right to point out that the voices of the majority of the people were stifled, however that stifling is especially that of the voices of the least powerful: the poor and women.

Christian feminist thinkers thus attribute the process of institutionalization to the influence of patriarchy, where within the institution of the Catholic Church ordained men now have exclusive access to the decision-making processes, the administrative power, and the functions of ordained ministry.

In Schillebeeckx's historical account of the development of the church's theology of ministry it is apparent that a process of institutionalization has brought about a more hierarchical and formalized structure than had existed in the earliest Christian community. In the more formalized institution, the prophetic and teaching roles are appropriated into the ordained leadership. In the early Christian community a person was appointed as minister to be a leader in the building up of the community, but by the medieval period, men were ordained principally in order to celebrate the Eucharist.[18] Certainly in the ancient Christian community, the one called as leader was the obvious person to preside at the Eucharist, but a significant shift occurred historically so that the celebration of the eucharist became a major focus in determining the meaning and function of the ordained minister.

14. Schillebeeckx, *Church with a Human Face*, 91–92.
15. Schillebeeckx, *Church with a Human Face*, 61.
16. Schillebeeckx, *Church with a Human Face*, 122.
17. Schillebeeckx, *Church with a Human Face*, 148.
18. Schillebeeckx, *Church with a Human Face*, 194.

The Hierarchical Ordering and Elevation

Schillebeeckx has argued that the hierarchical structuring of the ordained ministry has effectively become a vehicle of domination that hinders rather than helps the work of the church. It has served to emphasize the clergy/lay division and foster clericalism. Those higher in ranking in the hierarchy have power and juridical authority over the Christian community, on the basis of their status as ordained clergy rather than their relationship with the Christian community. A good argument can be made that the ordained members of the church ought not to have power *over* the rest of the baptized, nor should the church's ministry be understood as ranked or graded such that those higher in the hierarchy are understood to be greater than those below. That is not to say there ought not to be a threefold ministry but that the three roles of episcopacy, presbyterate, and diaconate can be understood alternatively as three mutual and equal aspects of the ministry of the church.

The hierarchical ordering of the ministry into "castes of clergy and laity"[19] has tended to further separate the work of the ordained ministry from mutual interaction and cooperation with the community. Those higher in the hierarchy are understood to have an elevated status. In addition, the ordained have a more elevated status than that of the rest of the baptized which, as I have already mentioned, contributes to a sense of powerlessness amongst the baptized people of God.

That the ordained ministry is understood to have an elevated status is evident from the liturgical texts for the ordination of bishops, priests, and deacons set out in the 1968 *Pontificale Romanorum*. As Mary Collins comments, these texts reflect the long tradition of the church "of making status distinctions within the community of believers and among those who serve it."[20] Collins cites numerous examples in which the language of the liturgy speaks of the elevation of the minister. Candidates to the diaconate are told, "you are being raised to the order of deacon."[21] Those to be ordained to the presbyterate are told, "you are now to be advanced to the order of the presbyterate."[22]

The status of the ordained is not only manifest in liturgical language but also in particular ritual symbols. Collins argues that power and status is established, maintained, and clarified in certain postures and in the

---

19. Ruether, *Woman-Church*, 75.
20. Collins, *Worship*, 137.
21. Pontificale Romanum, *De ordinatione diaconi*, 14.
22. Pontificale Romanum, *De ordinatione diaconi*, 14.

Part One—A Critique of the Traditional Theology

conferring of insignia such as garments, rings, or croziers.[23] "Controlling access to certain ritual spaces is another way of ritualizing power relationships,"[24] she contends. It is revealing to observe the symbolism of posture and stance of both the ordained minister and the congregation during the eucharistic liturgy. Sarah Ann Fairbanks also discusses how dominance is communicated by various postures, stances, and gestures in the liturgy such as, "who stands while others kneel; who gives the blessing while others bow their heads to receive it."[25] As Fairbanks and Collins both note, this pattern of dominance and subordination is held in place by a passive majority, who have little active role in the liturgy and generally do not challenge this pattern in any way. Furthermore, the fact that the proclamation of the gospel and the function of preaching in the liturgy is restricted to the ordained acts to consolidate this power structure. Catherine Hilkert draws attention to this in her recent publication on preaching:

> Restriction of the public proclamation of the gospel at the key moment of the community's celebration of its deepest identity—the eucharist—to ordained males suggests implicitly that men have a privileged hearing of the gospel, whether by divine plan or by church discipline.[26]

Clearly there can be no mistaking from the liturgical texts, nor from other gestures, symbols, and practices of the church, that the official stance of the contemporary Roman Catholic Church is that the ordained ministry has an elevated position. This elevated status acts to undermine and minimize the role of the rest of the baptized in the mission and ministry of the church.

It is surely the responsibility of all baptized persons to participate in decision-making procedures. It is not sufficient for the unordained baptized to simply receive decisions from the hierarchy. It is important that they participate in the making of those decisions or at least have adequate access to the decision-making procedures of the church. This does not happen today at an international level and not always at local levels. Margaret Ulloa observes this phenomenon, concluding that the centrality of the ordained priest is actually emphasized by the introduction of lay participation that does not share authority:

23. Collins, *Worship*, 102.
24. Collins, *Worship*, 102.
25. Fairbanks, "Liturgical Preaching by Women," 134.
26. Hilkert, *Naming Grace*, 164.

> Few indeed are the priests and bishops who are willing to accept parish councils and deanery meetings where the opinion of lay participants is given equal status with that of clerical participants, and fewer still those who have the courage to release any of their power in reality. As a result, the introduction of lay participation has in some ways served to underline the centrality of the ordained priest, and to reinforce the received notion that the functioning of the Church and most of our spiritual lives revolve around this essential sacred figure.[27]

Although lay involvement in the church has undoubtedly increased in recent years, one needs to ask whether this involvement is extended to the decision-making procedures of the church. Traditionally this has not been the case. In fact *Lumen Gentium* affirms that the laity "carry out their own part in the mission of the whole Christian people with respect to the Church and the world."[28] The document argues:

> A secular quality is proper and special to laymen . . . the laity, by their very vocation, seek the kingdom of God by engaging in temporal affairs and by ordering them according to the plan of God. They live in the world, that is, in each and in all of the secular professions and occupations. They live in the ordinary circumstances of family and social life, from which the very web of their existence is woven . . . They are called there by God . . . It is therefore his (the layman) special task to illumine and organize these (temporal) affairs . . .[29]

One can detect in this document a false division between the laity and the clergy. After all, even the clergy live in the world and have families and a social life. The ordained are not cut off from the world: they too must live, eat, and engage in temporal affairs and so ought to take responsibility in those affairs. Conversely, the baptized people of God are called to a commitment to the life of the church and must take their responsibility there. Hans Küng has drawn attention to this dilemma: "People like to talk of the participation of the laity in the *life* (not the decisions) of the church. They also like to speak of the participation of the laity in the decisions of the *world* (but not of the church). They do not at all like to speak, at least in official binding

---

27. Ulloa, "Extending Ordained Ministry," 5–6.
28. Abbott, *Documents of Vatican II*, 57.
29. Abbott, *Documents of Vatican II*, 57–58.

Part One—A Critique of the Traditional Theology

documents, of the participation of the laity in the *decisions* of the *church*."[30] Mary Hines voices a similar view as she comments upon John Paul II's conviction that the clergy should refrain from political involvement:

> The papal position reflects the increasingly problematic position that the laity is primarily responsible for the church's mission in the world, while clergy and members of religious communities are to attend to the church's inner life and its more institutional aspects . . . The Vatican II revisioning of the close relationship of church and world simply does not support a facile division of labor based on a prior structural classification of the members of the church into laity and clergy.[31]

Hines is right to critique the papal position. The prevention or even discouragement of ministers engaging in political life may result in the stifling of a prophetic voice. Prophets arise in various situations. They may be ordained or they may be quite remote from the church.

Letty Russell offers a solution to this dilemma when she argues that authority in the church ought to be grounded in the partnership of all the baptized people:

> The emerging feminist paradigm trying to make sense of biblical and theological truth claims is that of *authority as partnership* . . . Ordering is included through inclusion of diversity in a rainbow spectrum that does not require that persons submit to the "top" but, rather, that they participate in the common task of creating an interdependent community of humanity and nature. Authority is exercised in community and tends to reinforce ideas of co-operation, with contributions from a wide diversity of persons enriching the whole.[32]

A final aside that deserves comment is an issue that Schillebeeckx raises. He argues that the whole basis of this elevation of the priestly ministry lies in an understanding of Jesus's priesthood based in his divinity, rather than his humanity.[33] Schillebeeckx seems to argue for a theology of ordained ministry that is solely based in the humanity of Jesus, a point of view which I believe is also problematic: "[I]f the mediatorship of Jesus is located in his humanity, the priesthood of the church (which is a participation in the

30. Küng, "Participation of the Laity," 80.
31. Hines, "Community for Liberation," 166.
32. Russell, "Authority and the Challenge," 144.
33. Schillebeeckx, *Church with a Human Face*, 203.

The Hierarchical Ordering and Elevation

priesthood of Christ) indeed takes on a different significance and no less a truly sacramental significance."[34]

Whilst I applaud Schillebeeckx's critique of theologies of ministries that have failed to take sufficient account of the humanity of Jesus of Nazareth, I believe that both the humanity and divinity of Christ need to be held in tension in the search for a theological foundation for Christian ministry.

In *Christ,* Schillebeeckx restores the significance of the humanity of Jesus by drawing on the Letter to the Hebrews. Here Jesus is presented as high priest; a priesthood not in the Jewish sense, but rather "of another order" which critiques the levitical priesthood: "In the humanity of Jesus we see who and how God is," explains Schillebeeckx. Jesus is the visible expression of God, but he is also human as we are and shows solidarity with humankind.[35] What is observable in Hebrews, explains Schillebeeckx, is a demythologization of the Jewish notion of priesthood: "For the author, the love of the human Jesus who suffers for others, in faithfulness to God and in solidarity with the history of human suffering, is priesthood in the true sense of the word: bringing [humankind] to God."[36]

It is in this sense that Schillebeeckx understands Jesus as mediator between God and humankind. Jesus has undergone great suffering, and in fact makes the sacrifice of his own life in order to remain faithful to God, and in so doing opens up access to God for all of humankind in a new way. Thus the humanity of Jesus cannot be overlooked in our understanding of his priesthood, nor in our understanding of the common priesthood of all believers. It is difficult to derive an elevated view of the ordained ministry when ministry is theologically grounded in both the humanity and divinity of Jesus Christ.

Marie Isaacs takes the stance that the Epistle to the Hebrews subverts the Jewish cult, and that the demise of priesthood is the message of this text rather than merely its reinterpretation.[37] She demonstrates that there are other modes of access to God besides the priestly model depicted in Hebrews, such as that imagined in the entry into the Promised Land. "Here we are presented with a picture of the people of God as a community on the move; pilgrims journeying towards God."[38] She makes the aside, "unlike

---

34. Schillebeeckx, *Church with a Human Face,* 203.
35. Schillebeeckx, *Church with a Human Face,* 203.
36. Schillebeeckx, *Church with a Human Face,* 254.
37. Isaacs, "Priesthood," 58.
38. Isaacs, "Priesthood," 60.

the exclusive caste of priesthood, this band (Heb 11:1–40) includes not only men but women."[39] Hans Küng follows a similar line, suggesting that the message of the Epistle to the Hebrews is that Jesus fulfills and abolishes the priesthood of the Old Testament.[40] This indicates that one must take seriously the critique of the levitical priesthood outlined in the Epistle to the Hebrews. This critique is often overlooked in traditional theology: "The liturgy of the Church, however, sees in the priesthood of Aaron and the service of the Levites, as in the institution of the seventy elders, a prefiguring of the ordained ministry of the new Covenant."[41]

The life of the historical Jesus has in fact acted to critique the levitical priesthood in which "every priest stands day after day at his service, offering again and again the same sacrifices that can never take away sins" (Heb 10:11). Rather it is the life lived by Jesus in utter commitment to the realm of God and which finally resulted in his cruel death on a cross that is salvific. This is the sacrifice that is remembered and made present by the Christian community albeit through the leadership of the ordained minister.

---

39. Isaacs, "Priesthood," 60.
40. Küng, *Why Priests?* 29.
41. *Catechism of the Catholic Church*, 1541.

4

"Marked with a Special Character"

THE TRADITIONAL UNDERSTANDING OF the character bestowed by ordination asks too much of the sacrament of ordination and too little of the sacrament of baptism. The notion of ontological character has served to separate the ordained ministry from the Christian community. It has tended to detract from the significance and power of baptism and acts to create a false division between the ministerial priesthood and the common priesthood. The notion of the bestowal of a permanent and indelible spiritual character upon a minister at ordination does not convey meaning today. This is not to deny the new relationship with the Christian community into which the ordained person is brought, nor the special grace that is conferred with ordination, as with any of the church's sacramental actions.

The Vatican II document, *Presbyterorum Ordinis,* claims: "[T]he sacerdotal office of priests is conferred by that special sacrament through which priests, by the anointing of the Holy Spirit, are marked with a special character and are so configured to Christ the Priest that they can act in the person of Christ the Head."[1]

In the *Catechism of the Catholic Church* one finds further elaboration: "This sacrament configures the recipient to Christ by a special grace of the Holy Spirit, so that he may serve as Christ's instrument for his church."[2] The *Catechism* continues. ". . . The sacrament of holy orders, like the other

---

1. *Presbyterorum Ordinis,* para. 2 in Abbott, *Documents of Vatican II.*
2. *Catechism of the Catholic Church,* 1581,

two [baptism and confirmation], confers an *indelible spiritual character* and cannot be repeated or conferred temporarily."[3]

The *Catechism* also claims that an ordained person can be discharged from their duties, but not from their ordained status: "[H]e cannot become a layman again in the strict sense because the character imprinted by ordination is forever. The vocation and mission received on the day of his ordination mark him permanently."[4]

In his historical survey, Schillebeeckx challenges the setting of ordination "on a new ontological level"[5] over baptism. He argues that it is baptism that is "the ontological matrix and root of the sacrament of ordination" and it is baptism "which gives ordination its substance."[6] As a result of the way in which the doctrine of priestly character has functioned since the Council of Trent, he contends it has become "a burdensome heritage: [T]he character became the feature that isolated the priest from the church community... Since Trent, the character has also been made the key concept of the priestly ministry. The character became as it were the "ideology" of the priesthood."[7] Schillebeeckx prefers to interpret the character as the "charisma of the ministry"[8] that is given by the Spirit to the minister in order to serve the community. This pneumatological character of the ministry is foundational in his thinking.

The traditional understanding that ontological character is bestowed by ordination detracts from the significance of baptism. It is baptism, not ordination, that is the foundation for Christian ministry. Baptism is the sacrament signifying entry into the Christian community and as such is the foundation for all Christian discipleship. In this sense, baptism underpins the ministry of the church. Although few feminist scholars comment specifically on the notion of priestly character, most understand baptism to be the foundation for ministry. Marjorie Procter-Smith argues that baptism is both prophetic and empowering, and invites the community to "realize its own baptismal character as a community of equals in Christ."[9] She emphasizes the transforming prophetic and priestly demands that call the baptized

---

3. *Catechism of the Catholic Church*, 1582.
4. *Catechism of the Catholic Church*, 1583.
5. Schillebeeckx, *Church with a Human Face*, 205.
6. Schillebeeckx, *Church with a Human Face*, 205.
7. Schillebeeckx, *Church with a Human Face*, 233.
8. Schillebeeckx, *Church with a Human Face*, 233.
9. Procter-Smith, *In Her Own Rite*, 145.

person to engage "in continual struggle to bring the church and the world into harmony with the baptismal vision of equality."[10] *The Catechism of the Catholic Church* itself affirms that it is baptism that configures the baptized to Christ: "It [Baptism] signifies and actually brings about death to sin and entry into the life of the Most Holy Trinity through configuration to the Paschal mystery of Christ."[11]

Ordination, on the other hand, can be understood as the sacramental acknowledgement of a particular relationship that the minister has with the Christian community. Through baptism the Christian already has a particular relationship with the risen Christ, but through ordination a further crystallization of that relationship is being affirmed. It is a relationship in which the person's gift of leadership is offered for the good of the Christian community.

Even though special grace is conferred at ordination, the language of ontological change or indelibility is not helpful. Undoubtedly, the sacraments and rituals of the church carry the power to transform. The sacrament of marriage, for example, is at one level celebrating a decision between two people to commit themselves to one another. But as Catherine Hilkert writes, the power of naming such a commitment acts to deepen that which is signified in words: "A friendship forms before it is fully recognized and claimed, but when friends or partners explicitly claim the bond of love between them, they also deepen their commitment to one another and make decisions that will affect future choices."[12]

Likewise in the rite of ordination, the explicit commitment to the ministry of leadership and to a particular relationship with the community can be deepened by the power of the sacrament itself, now publicly affirmed and proclaimed. In this way, special grace can be conferred upon the ordained through the sacrament that might assist the minister in their commitment to the Christian community. The ordained person is committing to a new relationship to the Christian community and so becomes accountable to that community.

The notion of a special grace conferred does not imply that special status ought to be attached to this ministry and nor does it signify a sacred power apart from that of the gathered community. Furthermore, to go beyond the acknowledgement of a special grace conferred by ordination to

---

10. Procter-Smith, *In Her Own Rite*, 145–46.
11. *Catechism of the Catholic Church*, 1239.
12. Hilkert, *Naming Grace*, 47.

propose an "indelible character" serves to make a false distinction between the ordained and the whole of the baptized community and consolidates the elevated status of the ordained.

Luther criticized the notion of indelible character in the sixteenth century, recognizing its capacity to detract from the significance of baptism:

> [T]hey have nevertheless invented "characters" which they [Catholic Church] attribute to this sacrament of theirs and which are indelibly impressed on those who are ordained. Whence do such ideas come, I ask? ... They have sought by this means to set up a seedbed of implacable discord, by which clergy and laymen should be separated from each other farther than heaven and earth, to the incredible injury of the grace of baptism and to the confusion of our fellowship in the gospel. ... According to what the Scriptures teach us, what we call the priesthood is a ministry. So I cannot understand at all why one who has been made a priest cannot again become a layman; for the sole difference between him and a layman is his ministry.[13]

The notion that ordination so marks a person that "the character imprinted is forever"[14] is questionable. I will argue shortly that ordination ought not be understood as a *necessarily* lifelong commitment.

The tradition of the Roman Catholic Church has connected the notion of character with the unrepeatability of ordination: "The sacrament of Holy Orders, like the other two, confers an *indelible spiritual character* and cannot be repeated or conferred temporarily."[15]

However, the notion of character has also served to separate the ordained minister from the Christian community. It has often been invoked as a foundation for an elevated ontological status for the ordained. The notion of ontological character focuses particularly upon the minister, taking little account of the relationship between that minister and the Christian community.

The traditional teaching of the indelible character of the ordained minister, along with the teaching that the sacraments act *ex opere operato*,[16] assures the Christian community that if an ordained minister is unworthy then the sacraments are not made invalid. The church argues this on the

---

13. Luther, *Three Treatises*, 242–49.
14. *Catechism of the Catholic Church*, 1583.
15. *Catechism of the Catholic Church*, 1582.
16. *Catechism of the Catholic Church*, 1128.

grounds that the ordained person is configured to Christ through ordination and so it is Christ who acts in the sacraments. I agree that it is indeed the case that the sacraments remain valid. However I would argue that the presiding minister is configured to Christ, but by virtue of baptism rather than ordination. Furthermore, in any of the sacramental actions of the church, it is always Christ that acts in the midst of the community. Both the ordained minister and the baptized community cooperate with the presence and activity of God in their midst: they do not affect the sacraments themselves. However, there is a danger that in our enthusiasm to establish the validity of the sacraments, the church can overlook too easily the turmoil and distress caused when an ordained person is either grossly incompetent or acts immorally. The unworthiness of an ordained minister, whilst it does not put into question the validity of the sacraments, is nevertheless an issue that should not be minimized. Extreme incompetence or the gross immorality of ministers needs to be faced and addressed by the Christian community.

To summarize: the language of indelible character and ontological change is not helpful and serves rather to detract from the significance of baptism which is the foundation for Christian ministry.

5

The Symbolic Role of the Priesthood

AN UNDERSTANDING OF THE representational role of the ordained minister can contribute to a view of the ordained ministry as "set apart." I want to critique the traditional notion that the ordained minister primarily represents Christ, and only indirectly represents the church. The traditional notion is deficient because it focuses upon the person of the minister outside of the context of the Christian community.

The Catechism of the Catholic Church states, "The priest, by virtue of the sacrament of Holy Orders, acts *in persona Christi Capitis*."[1] The ministerial priesthood also represents the church, and claims the official position, *because* it represents Christ. This official view of the nature of the ordained ministry has also been outlined in the Vatican II document, *Presbyterorum Ordinis*: "[T]he sacerdotal office of priests is conferred by that special sacrament through which priests, by the anointing of the Holy Spirit, are marked with a special character and are so configured to Christ the priest that they can act in the person of Christ the Head."[2]

The 1976 *Declaration on the Question of the Admission of Women to the Ministerial Priesthood* affirmed this line of argument: "[T]he bishop or priest, in the exercise of his ministry, does not act in his own name, *in persona propria*: he represents Christ who acts through him: 'The priest truly acts in the place of Christ.'"[3]

---

1. *Catechism of the Catholic Church*, 1548.
2. *Presbyterorum Ordinis*, para. 2 in Abbott, *Documents of Vatican II.*
3. Sacred Congregation for the Clergy, *Inter Insigniores*, 12.

The Symbolic Role of the Priesthood

The Declaration continues on to define the notion of *in persona Christi* as "taking the role of Christ, to the point of being his very image, when he pronounces the words of consecration."[4] Later it is added that the priest represents the church:

> [T]he priest . . . equally represents the church: he acts in her name with "the intention of doing what she does." In this sense the theologians of the Middle Ages said that the minister also acts in persona Ecclesiae, that is to say, in the name of the whole church and in order to represent her.[5]

I oppose the traditional view that the ordained minister alone represents Christ and then in an indirect way represents the church.[6] In this view, the ordained minister is interpreted in relation to Christ in isolation from the context of the Christian community and disconnected from the representative role with respect to the church.

Although Edward Schillebeeckx rightly critiques the notion that the ordained ministry is a representation of the one priesthood of Christ "over against the Christian community,"[7] his discussion about any representational role of the ordained ministry does not offer much assistance since it remains scant and ambiguous. He leans towards a purely functional understanding of the ordained ministry in much of his writing.[8] However, in his discussion of the documents of Vatican II, he comments upon what he sees as confusion in statements about the representation of Christ. He argues that the documents of the Second Vatican Council sometimes locate this representation "in the minister as a person and not formally in the act of exercising of his office."[9] He claims, "at all events, the representation of Christ comes about not purely on the basis of ministry . . ."[10] Here Schillebeeckx seems to be moving away from a functional view of ministry to the acknowledgment of a representational role for the ordained minister. However he does not enlarge upon this. What is certain in Schillebeeckx's discussion is that the ordained ministry is founded in the ontological baptism of the Spirit.

4. Sacred Congregation for the Clergy, *Inter Insigniores*, 12.
5. Sacred Congregation for the Clergy, *Inter Insigniores*, 12.
6. *Catechism of the Catholic Church*, 1553.
7. Schillebeeckx, *Church with a Human Face*, 213.
8. Schillebeeckx, *Church with a Human Face*, 157.
9. Schillebeeckx, *Church with a Human Face*, 206.
10. Schillebeeckx, *Church with a Human Face*, 206.

Part One—A Critique of the Traditional Theology

Many feminist theologians have been either silent or dismissive around the questions of the symbolic function of the ordained ministry. For example, Lynn Rhodes's simplistic claim, "the clergyperson is no more a 'representative' than anyone else who identifies with the community" does not allow for the possibility that the ordained minister might have a role of representing the wider church to the local community and the local community to the wider church.[11] Mary Daly, for example, adopted the position of a purely functional understanding of the ordained ministry when she dismissed the possibility of a symbolic role for the ordained:

> When the emphasis is shifted away from symbolic roles which are identified with fixed states of life and toward functional roles freely assumed on the basis of personal qualifications and skills, away from caste systems and toward specialization based on ability, there will be hope for realization of that higher level of dialogue and cooperation between men and women which we seek.[12]

Daly's view unnecessarily linked a symbolic role to a "fixed state of life," and did not allow for any kind of symbolic role for the ordained ministry. She rightly acknowledged that many ministerial tasks can be taken on by skilled members of the community, but failed to see any distinct role for an ordained ministry. For Rosemary Ruether too, authentic ministerial leadership is functional:

> A ministry of function, rather than of clerical caste, can allow the true plurality of the ministerial needs of the community to be met... A community based on the ministry of function values and supports the talents of its members and knows how to empower these talents and to use them to develop the talents of others.[13]

And yet Ruether's understanding, like Schillebeeckx's, is not purely functional. She argues that designating the leadership role to one person for a certain period of time serves the purpose of symbolizing the unity of the community. The leader then "sums up the redemptive life of the community in its symbolic unity."[14] This symbolic function of the ordained minister is not further explained nor developed in Ruether's ecclesiology but

---

11. Rhodes, *Co-creating*, 114.
12. Daly, *Church and the Second Sex*, 208.
13. Ruether, *Women-Church*, 89–90.
14. Ruether, *Women-Church*, 91.

remains as a faint suggestion of a more than functional role in the ministry of leadership.

Whilst I argue that the traditional notion that the ordained minister primarily represents Christ is in need of critique, I do not advocate a purely functional understanding of the ordained ministry. The functions of ministry, tasks such as teaching, preaching, healing, and administration, are works that are pastoral, political, and prophetic and can be undertaken by those gifted, whether ordained or not. These functional tasks are not the hallmark or sole realm of the ordained. Susan Ross puts forward a convincing case that the sacraments ought to be understood symbolically rather than instrumentally. She explores what the symbol represents rather than adopting a purely functional approach, claiming that a functional approach runs the risk of separating the sacrament from personal and ecclesial dimensions.[15] I suggest that there is a distinct symbolic role required of the ordained ministry, which is to act *in persona ecclesiae*, that is to act as a representative of the church. Later I show that the ministerial priesthood has a distinctive representational role, but one which also illustrates its intrinsic relationship to the Christian community.

A helpful way to redress the historical loss of connection between the ordained ministry and the Christian community is to ask the question: How is the ministerial priesthood *related* to the Christian community? This is a prior question to the oft-asked, "How is the ministerial priesthood *distinct* from the priesthood of all the baptized?" As I demonstrated above, the church has proclaimed that the ministerial priesthood stands *in persona Christi,* representing Christ. Since I argue that all of the baptized are called to this role, I do not dispute this claim. However, I resist any distinction between lay and ordained ministers that rests in "the identification of the ordained minister as standing *in persona Christi* over and against the lay baptized."[16] Wood rightly argues, "there is a sense in which each baptized Christian can be understood to be configured to Christ and to stand *in persona Christi*."[17] All of the baptized are indeed called to act *in persona Christi,* and to be an instrument for the work of Christ. Dennis Ferrara argues that Thomas Aquinas was responsible for the axiom *in persona Christi,* and understood this in an instrumental sense. The minister allowed Christ to work through him despite his own unworthiness or

---

15. Ross, "God's Embodiment," 188–89.
16. Wood, "Priestly Identity," 111.
17. Wood, "Priestly Identity," 112.

otherness from Christ. Ferrara demonstrates that the notion that the minister must resemble Christ (for example, to be male, as Jesus was male), is not in keeping with Aquinas's use of the phrase. Rather "the priest is but the instrument through whom Christ himself speaks here and now," and does not have to resemble Christ or "represent him visibly or externally."[18] This is, of course, not the understanding expressed by the Declaration on the Question of the Admission of Women to the Ministerial priesthood which argues for a physical resemblance to Christ (thus maleness is essential) and which interprets Aquinas in this way.

The implications of failing to recognize that each baptized person is invited to stand *in persona Christi* are profound for women. *Inter Insigniores* claimed that a woman could not be ordained because she could not represent Christ. The document reasoned that if a woman were ordained, "it would be difficult to see in the minister the image of Christ."[19] This was a simplistic and insulting claim, reducing Christ to a male historical figure and ignoring the message of the gospel that all are made in the image of God.

Edward Kilmartin shares the view that the baptized represent Christ when he argues, "the priesthood of all believers is another form of representation of Christ . . . one cannot situate the peculiarity of ordained ministry in the unqualified concept of representation of Christ."[20] However I am not persuaded by Kilmartin's view that the priesthood of all the faithful is "another form" of representing Christ, but rather that it is the one vocation of all of the baptized to represent Christ to others. However the question remains as to what is the distinguishing feature of the ordained ministry. I will show in a later chapter that the distinctive role of the ordained ministry is that of representing the church in a twofold sense: the minister represents the local community to the wider church and also represents the wider church to the local community.

Susan Wood argues that this sacramental representation of the community can be understood as the representation of Christ, the head, to the community (*in persona Christi capitis*). All of the baptized are called to be representatives of Christ, but because of a particular relationship between the ordained minister and the community, she claims, the minister fulfills a distinctive role standing *in persona Christi capitis*. Although Wood is

18. Ferrara, "Representation or Self-effacement?," 195–224.
19. Sacred Congregation for the Clergy, *Inter Insigniores*, sec. 5.
20. Kilmartin, "Apostolic Office," 250.

The Symbolic Role of the Priesthood

careful to add that the headship of the ordained minister is one of representation and not one of domination, I am not convinced by her argument. The image of headship can suggest a hierarchy that sets one ordained person over and against the Christian community. Dennis Ferrara critiques this interpretation of the ordained minister for similar reasons:

> In this new interpretation, which is especially developed by *Inter insigniores,* the consecrating priest is viewed as representing Christ *as* Head of the Church (*in persona Christi* as *in persona Christi capitis*), so that the priestly act of consecrating the Eucharist emerges as an act of hierarchical power.[21]

In situations where the community is governed and cared for collaboratively by a team of both ordained and non-ordained ministers, the image of the ordained minister as standing *in persona Christi capitis* seems out of place. All of the baptized stand *in persona Christi* to one another, and the ordained ministers who represent the church stand *in persona ecclesia* on behalf of both their local community and the universal church. The role of representing the church should not be understood as a secondary or indirect role. Edward Kilmartin has rightly argued that "outside the ecclesial context, apostolic office cannot represent Christ."[22] He argues that the faith of the Christian community is a prerequisite for the ordained minister's role in representing Christ, and so cannot be considered to be prior to the minister's role of representing the church. I would add that our call to represent Christ to others is derived from our baptism into the Christian community.

The notion that the ordained minister *primarily* represents Christ to the community or *alone* represents Christ is therefore inadequate. To interpret the role of the ordained minister apart from the community acts to consolidate division between the ordained and non-ordained members of the church.

THE ORDAINED MINISTRY: A LIFE-LONG COMMITMENT?

Flowing from the notion that the ordained are stamped with an indelible character at the moment of their ordination is the traditional understanding

---

21. Ferrara, "Representation or Self-effacement?," 197.
22. Kilmartin, "Apostolic Office," 260.

that this commitment will be irrevocable and lifelong. Such an understanding exists despite the now numerous examples of ordained ministers leaving the ministry and even being removed from priestly duties through irresponsible, immoral, or criminal behavior. I suggest that the ordained ministry need not be a lifelong commitment.

In his historical overview of ministry, Schillebeeckx notes that in the early church there was no distinction between the leadership of community and the power of ordination, so that "a minister who for any personal reason ceased to be the president of a community *ipso facto* returned to being a layman (sic) in the full sense of the word."[23] He argues that the notion of an indelible priestly character was unknown at this time. Schillebeeckx proposes a rather functional view of the ordained ministry and does not hold with the notion of ontological priestly character, or with the necessity for a lifelong commitment to the ordained ministry.

Few feminist scholars have commented on this aspect of the ordained ministry. Nevertheless, it seems self-evident after a critique of the notion of ontological character that there remains no reason to insist upon a lifelong commitment. In circumstances where both the minister and the Christian community understand the person as having left the ministry of the church, then that person is surely no longer an official minister of the church. And yet the teaching of the church remains:

> It is true that someone validly ordained can, for a just reason, be discharged from the obligations and functions linked to ordination, or can be forbidden to exercise them; but he cannot become a layman again in the strict sense, because the character imprinted by ordination is for ever.[24]

When ordained ministers leave the ordained ministry, they no longer perform the functions of ministry or leadership. Furthermore, when a minister ceases to lead a community he or she no longer fulfills the symbolic function of representing that community to the wider church. If the relationship of a minister to a community is severed, the minister can no longer represent the universal church to that community.[25] Despite no longer performing any practical or symbolic role, such a person is nevertheless understood to

---

23. Schillebeeckx, *Ministry*, 41.
24. *Catechism of the Catholic Church*, 1583.
25. I do not include here the example of retired ordained ministers who, whilst they no longer function in a practical way by leading a community, still relate to the Christian community. They function symbolically, representing the church to the community.

have been ontologically and irrevocably altered by ordination. What this means is very unclear, particularly in the case of one forbidden to act as a priest because of misconduct. The church's teaching is that the indelible character conferred at ordination configures the recipient to Christ by a special grace "so that he may serve as Christ's instrument for his church."[26] And yet the dismissed person no longer serves the church as a priest.

Whilst there are many good reasons for lifelong commitment to the ordained ministry, there also needs to be the possibility of not making such a commitment for life. Miroslav Volf, who also argues that a calling to ministry should not be *necessarily* a lifelong affair, proposes that our knowledge of the charismata of ministry must be viewed as provisional:

> We do not know whether a person will have a certain charisma in the future as well . . . Because the activity of the Spirit is unpredictable and because our human knowledge of the activity of the Spirit is limited, any (formal or informal) ecclesial acknowledgement that a certain person has a certain charisma must always remain subject to revision.[27]

When a commitment to ministry is made that is not necessarily a lifelong commitment, there is room to accommodate the acknowledgement of our provisional understanding of the charismata. It may well be of course that many ministers do in fact remain in ministry throughout their life, but, in my view, there needs to be the possibility of not doing so.

A consequence of the church teaching of the irrevocable nature of ordination is that ordained ministers who leave the ministry of the Roman Catholic Church—perhaps to marry—often feel shamed by the church and find it difficult to move into a new phase of their life with integrity and hope. Some of these men have in fact not wished to leave the ordained ministry but are forced to do so because they are unable to accept the requirement of celibacy. Others do wish to leave and perhaps for these latter men there is a need for formal acknowledgement in a liturgical context of their service to the ordained ministry and their movement into a new direction. For the well-being of both minister and community, I suggest that ordained persons who choose to marry ought to be able to continue their ministry as before.

---

26. *Catechism of the Catholic Church*, 1581.
27. Volf, *After Our Likeness*, 244.

6

The Mystification of the Eucharist

THE MYSTIFICATION OF THE Eucharist that arose during the medieval period and persisted into the twentieth century has contributed to the elevated status of ordained ministers and acts to disempower the rest of the baptized community.

Schillebeeckx notes that the perception of the Eucharist changed from the time of the early church when it was understood as a sacramental celebration that "makes the sacrifice of the cross present."[1] During the Middle Ages, however, a more elevated understanding developed which viewed the Eucharist more as "a *renewal* of the sacrifice of the cross."[2] It is interesting to note that even the term *sacerdos*, or its Greek equivalent *hiereus*, began to be used in the third century to speak of the presbyters.[3] These terms signify the one who is set aside for the cultic practices of prayer and sacrifice. Hans Küng emphatically claims, "the eucharistic celebration is not itself a sacrifice, but, ever and again, it refers to the unique sacrifice of Christ on the Cross, which through it becomes present and operative."[4] As the Epistle to the Hebrews exhorts, Jesus's sacrifice was once for all and further sacrifice is unnecessary and contrary to the message of this text (Heb 10:11–14).

---

1. Schillebeeckx, *Church with a Human Face*, 159.
2. Schillebeeckx, *Church with a Human Face*, 159.
3. Although in the ancient Christian communities many ministries were referred to, including apostles, prophets, presbyters, teachers, healers, deacons, evangelists, pastors and benefactors, the term "priest" was not used. Schillebeeckx, *Church with a Human Face*, 60.
4. Küng, *Why Priests?* 50.

A view of the Eucharist as *renewing* the sacrifice of the cross distances the ordained minister from the community. The presider at the Eucharist who becomes, in this context, the priest carrying out the renewed sacrifice is elevated in status and power. I claim that the ordained minister together with the gathered community remembers and makes present the sacrifice of Jesus's life upon the cross. They do not in any way make sacrifice anew.

Rosemary Radford Ruether describes the elevation of the Eucharist into a symbol of power:

> [I]t is a matter of elevating this simple symbolic act of blessing and giving food and drink into the symbol of the power to control divine or redeeming life, a power that the clergy claim to possess in a way that is beyond the access of lay or merely "natural" human beings.[5]

In fact, asserts Ruether, the act of blessing and administering food and drink, unlike other skills of ministry, requires very few special talents. "Yet it is precisely this act which the clerical ministry has most stringently reserved for itself to express its exclusive power to transcend the community."[6] Ruether may be in danger here of undervaluing the signification of the eucharistic meal, and yet I believe she rightly questions the rigorous restriction by the Roman Catholic Church on who is authorized to perform this function in the liturgy.

Schüssler Fiorenza describes a simplicity in the eucharistic table ministry also, gleaned from her reading of the Acts of the Apostles, and suggests that it included "preparation of a meal, purchase and distribution of food, actual serving during the meal, and probably cleaning up afterwards."[7] This, Schüssler Fiorenza recalls, took place "day by day": "Day by day, as they spent much time together in the temple, they broke bread at home and ate their food with glad and generous hearts (Acts 2:46)."

James Dunn notes in his Foreword to Anne Primavesi and Jennifer Henderson's work, "it has been control of the sacred food which has been the secret of priestly power and privilege."[8] Primavesi and Henderson construct their argument around "the non-elevated status of Jesus' own breaking of bread,"[9] and argue convincingly that Jesus's inclusive table fellowship was

---

5. Ruether, *Women-Church*, 78.
6. Ruether, *Women-Church*, 90.
7. Fiorenza, *In Memory of Her*, 165.
8. Fiorenza, *In Memory of Her*, viii.
9. Primavesi and Henderson, *Our God Has No Favorites*, 15.

a "scandalously indiscriminate identification with sinners."[10] They suggest that the community itself must reclaim its eucharistic power in the eucharistic celebration: "All ask for the Spirit; all are changed through union with the Spirit; all pray to be gathered in unity; all pray for the transformation of the bread and wine into the body and blood of Christ; all partake of it and of the one Spirit."[11]

Pertinent to this discussion is Schillebeeckx's observation that no strong connection is made in the Christian Scriptures between the ministry of the church and presiding at the Eucharist, although he concludes that those competent to lead the community would also have been *ipso facto* presiders at the Eucharist.[12] Susan Wood notes the same point and suggests that the silence of the Scriptures on this matter is strong evidence that in fact there was no ministry that had presiding at the eucharistic meal as its main function. She suggests that "whoever prayed the eucharistic prayer did so as the natural expression of what they already were within the community."[13] Whilst the practices of the early church are not to be understood as prescriptive for today, the knowledge of a less mystified eucharistic meal—in which no rigid connection seems to have been made between presiding at the meal and the ministry of the church—can inform our vision of the ordained ministry today.

The gulf between the ordained clergy and the people was highlighted, claim Primavesi and Henderson, in the private masses of the medieval period, where "the cleric was indispensable, the laity was not."[14] Primavesi and Henderson enlarge upon this separation of the ordained minister from the community:

> The effect on the clergy of living behind these barricades is incalculable . . . The effect on the laity individually is more obvious. Made to feel dispensable, they dispense themselves from attendance . . . Congregations in the mainstream churches dwindle . . . The community withers, and eventually dies.[15]

The eucharistic meal, although sacred and transformative, is not an act of magic. Ruether's "simple symbolic act of blessing and giving food and drink"

10. Primavesi and Henderson, *Our God Has No Favorites*, 40.
11. Primavesi and Henderson, *Our God Has No Favorites*, 68.
12. Schillebeeckx, *Church with a Human Face*, 119–20.
13. Wood, "Priestly Identity," 115.
14. Primavesi and Henderson, *Our God Has No Favorites*, 70.
15. Primavesi and Henderson, *Our God Has No Favorites*, 71–72.

barely recognizes the sacred and central significance of the Eucharist as the meal in which Christ becomes present through the faith of the believing community. Primavesi and Henderson, on the other hand, although saying little about the role of the ordained minister, do recognize the signification of the eucharistic elements in their statement: "[A]ll pray for the transformation of the bread and wine into the body and blood of Christ; all partake of it and of the one Spirit."[16] Clearly, there is a sacred power at work in this liturgical act, but it is lodged amongst the gathered community and not solely in the hands of the ordained minister. The transformation of bread and wine into the body and blood of Christ is the result of the inspiration and action of God amongst and with the believing community. The sacred action of God amongst the believing community must not be undervalued, but neither must the eucharistic act be understood as the magical work or renewed sacrifice conducted by an ordained minister.

An elevated understanding of the Eucharist serves to further elevate the status of the ordained minister. But conversely, the way the church deals with the present-day shortage of priests can actually act to consolidate an elevated understanding of the Eucharist. Ann Graff comments on this dilemma:

> The community who has a minister, not a priest, cannot celebrate Eucharist fully because the minister is not institutionally authorized to consecrate. That church has to bring in either a priest or consecrated bread. These options endanger our understanding of the Eucharist and tend to qualify the blessing of the bread as a quasi-magical act. This problem argues for a more inclusive ordained ministry in the interest of the spiritual welfare of the church.[17]

Schillebeeckx makes similar remarks in the opening to *The Church with a Human Face*:

> Moreover, in all areas we can see an increasing shortage of priests. These facts often have serious consequences where traditional views are maintained. The Sunday celebration of the eucharist is trivialized (the laity preside over a kind of pseudo-eucharist, with hosts which are brought from elsewhere; this both takes the heart out of the celebration that in fact takes place and regards consecrated hosts in a magical way).[18]

---

16. Primavesi and Henderson, *Our God Has No Favorites*, 68.
17. Graff, "Women in the Roman Catholic Ministry," 228.
18. Schillebeeckx, *Church with a Human Face*, 1.

Schillebeeckx also critiques situations in which those who minister to the sick and dying are not able to offer a sacramental ministry which should rightfully accompany the visiting, that is, listening and being present: "[T]hose who have to accompany the sick to their deaths have abruptly to hand over the sacramental sealing of this whole process to a strange priest summoned from elsewhere—to the disillusionment of the dying person."[19]

It is problematic for church communities that those who are authorized as ministers, although they are not ordained, are unable to share in the liturgical and sacramental ministry. This situation highlights the separation of the liturgy from the life of the community, when in fact the liturgy of the community ought to ritualize the ongoing life of the community.

THE SACRED POWER OF THE ORDAINED MINISTER

I am in agreement with Edward Schillebeeckx and a number of feminist theologians in critiquing the notion that the ordained minister holds a sacred power. Whilst I do not deny that sacred power is at work in the Christian community and preeminently in the celebration of the Eucharist, I suggest that this power is made manifest amongst the gathered community rather than in the hands of one minister.

Although the scholastic notion of the sacred power *(sacra potestas)* of the ordained is given less weight than the notion of service[20] in the documents of Vatican II, there still exists a suggestion that sacred power is a quality that belongs to the ordained minister over and against the Christian community. I argue that this notion of *sacra potestas* assists in holding in place the elevated status of the ordained ministry. *Lumen Gentium* for example, comments: "The ministerial priest, by the sacred power he enjoys, molds and rules the priestly people. Acting in the person of Christ, he brings about the Eucharistic sacrifice, and offers it to God in the name of all people."[21]

Schillebeeckx has traced the development of the notion of sacred power by virtue of ordination, in which an ordained person has "priestly

---

19. Schillebeeckx, *Church with a Human Face*, 265.

20. In general in the *Lumen Gentium* document, the term power, *potestas,* is used less frequently than in documents of the earlier councils. The term seems to have been replaced by the notion of the work of service (*ministeria* or *munera*).

21. *Lumen Gentium,* 10, in Abbott, *Documents of Vatican II,* 27.

power in his own person,"[22] a power not dependent upon his appointment to a community. Priests now can celebrate the Eucharist on their own, explains Schillebeeckx, a notion "inconceivable" in the early church.

The above excerpt from *Lumen Gentium* implies that the ordained minister has both the power of jurisdiction and the power of consecration. He both rules the people and he brings about the eucharistic sacrifice. Feminist scholars rightly question such power, strongly critiquing a leadership in which decision-making power or teaching authority is lodged in any one person, rather than shared in the community. Feminist critique shifts attention from the "sacred power" of the ordained minister to the significance of the gathered community.

In the celebration of the Eucharist, whilst it may be the liturgical leader who invokes the power of God, who invites the faithful to prayer, or who performs the action of breaking bread, the power of the sacred is apprehended or made manifest *amongst the gathered community*. Anne Primavesi and Jennifer Henderson emphasize the communal nature of the Eucharist, in which all members of the community pray for the transformation of the bread and wine into the body and blood of Christ. "[The] invocation of the Spirit is the moment of real eucharistic power," argue Anne Primavesi and Jennifer Henderson, "the moment the community must reclaim."[23]

Susan Ross argues in a similar vein:

> A feminist eucharistic theology has its center in the ecclesial assembly not in the presider. When the focus is on the assembly, the Eucharist is a lavish gift to be shared, not scarce gold to be parceled out piecemeal only to those who qualify. Like the multiplication of the loaves and fishes, the eucharistic feast ought to be a living symbol of the openness and generosity of the Christian community. That it so often fails to live up to this generosity is a scandal.[24]

Thus the sacred power of God, manifest through the sacraments of the church and preeminently in the Eucharist, is not contained in the hands of one person but is apprehended in the gathered community, that is, in the presiding minister together with all of the baptized community. "For where two or three are gathered in my name, I am there among them" (Matt 18:20).

---

22. Schillebeeckx, *Church with a Human Face*, 193.
23. Primavesi and Henderson, *Our God Has No Favorites*, 68.
24. Ross, "God's Embodiment and Women," 204–5.

7

The Requirement of Celibacy for Ordained Ministry

THE REQUIREMENT OF CELIBACY for the ordained ministry has hindered the ministry of the Christian Church in that it has reduced the number of ministers who can be considered for ordination and has acted to further distance the ordained ministry from the Christian community.

In his commentary on the 1971 Synod of Bishops, Schillebeeckx advocates the ordination of married men to the priesthood. He argues that the charisma of celibacy can only act as a sign to the world if the obligatory connection between the ordained ministry and celibacy is removed. When celibacy is not freely chosen, but required of ordained ministers, celibacy "loses its authentic force as a sign."[1] Schillebeeckx records the remarks of one bishop at the Synod who lamented, "if we do not impose the charisma of celibacy by law, it will not be put into practice."[2] Schillebeeckx's response is simply, "here we can see the bankruptcy of the ideal which disguises other concerns."[3] Although the understanding in the church today is that only those who are prepared to freely embrace celibacy are ordained, this view does not take into account any psychological pressure upon ordinands to acquiesce to this requirement in response to their fundamental vocation to ministry, nor does it take into account the possibility that an ordained

---

1. Schillebeeckx, *Church with a Human Face*, 223.
2. Schillebeeckx, *Church with a Human Face*, 226.
3. Schillebeeckx, *Church with a Human Face*, 226

The Requirement of Celibacy for Ordained Ministry

person, having freely embraced celibacy in their youth, might in the context of later relationships regret the lifelong nature of this choice.

In his return to the data of the tradition, Schillebeeckx notes the presence of both married and unmarried ministers in the early church and he cites the requirement of ritual purity as the reason for the imposition of temporary laws of abstinence in the late fourth century.[4] Ute Ranke-Heinemann, like Schillebeeckx, notes that liturgical laws forbidding sexual intercourse before presiding at the Eucharist have a long history. Even in pre-Christian times, pagan priests practised abstinence or even castration in order to be "pure and holy mediators between the people and the god or goddess."[5] Although the increasing tendency in the Christian tradition for priests to celebrate the Eucharist daily meant that permanent abstinence from intercourse became a requirement, it was not until the twelfth century that the law of celibacy for ordained ministers was enforced and marriage prohibited. In his historical review, Schillebeeckx asks: "how could Christians again allow the force of ancient laws of purity when Jesus and the New Testament writers revoked the ritual precepts of the Old Testament and declared them void?"[6] At the origins of the requirement of celibacy, Schillebeeckx argues: "we find an antiquated anthropology and an ancient view of sexuality." He suggests that this ancient view, held by Christians and pagans alike, is expressed simply and bluntly by Jerome: "sexual intercourse is impure."[7] It is understandable that Schillebeeckx maintains that there are further pastoral reasons why the requirement of celibacy ought to be revised. The right of Christian communities to ministers and to the celebration of the Eucharist ought not to be hindered by this requirement, for the building up of the community is a "more urgent right."[8] A choice ought to be possible for ordained ministers, he suggests, for "what is better for one is less good and perhaps even oppressive for another."[9]

There seems to be unanimity amongst feminist thinkers that celibacy ought not to be a requirement for ordained ministry. For example, Margaret

---

4. Schillebeeckx, *Church with a Human Face*, 241.

5. Ranke-Heinemann, *Eunuchs for the Kingdom*, 99.

6. Schillebeeckx, *Church with a Human Face*, 242. I find Schillebeeckx's remark here somewhat insensitive to Judaism and needing to be relativized. Perhaps for Christians this is true.

7. Schillebeeckx, *Church with a Human Face*, 243.

8. Schillebeeckx, *Church with a Human Face*, 248.

9. Schillebeeckx, *Church with a Human Face*, 247.

Ulloa comments that with increasing numbers of married convert priests accepted as Catholic priests she finds it "impossible to take seriously any argument in favour of compulsory celibacy."[10] Jane Dempsey Douglas follows Calvin in suggesting that celibacy is a grace "rather than a state that can be achieved by human discipline," arguing "it should be practised with the expectation that its need may be temporary, rather than on the basis of a lifelong vow."[11]

However, the starting point for reflection amongst many feminist thinkers differs from that of Schillebeeckx. In their discussions on celibacy, feminist thinkers point to a long tradition within Catholicism of not only devaluing human sexuality but also of demonizing female sexuality. In this regard they push the historical exploration of celibacy to deeper roots than does Schillebeeckx. I believe that the insights of feminist thinkers must be taken very seriously, for their judgments—arising out of the experience of being female—are sensitive to unwarranted and prejudiced attacks on women. Ruether recalls the words of Tertullian in her efforts to expose a deeply-rooted depreciation of women:

> You are the Devil's Gateway. It is you who plucked the fruit of the forbidden tree. You are the first who deserted the divine law. You are the one who persuaded him whom even the Devil was not strong enough to attack. All too easily you destroyed the image of God, man. Because of your desert, that is death, even the Son of God had to die . . . Therefore cover your head and your figure with sack-cloth and ashes.[12]

Ute Ranke-Heinemann's *Eunuchs for the Kingdom of Heaven* is a detailed account of the disparagement of women and human sexuality throughout the Catholic tradition. She cites the origins of the suspicion towards human sexuality in antiquity: "The sexual act was thought of as dangerous, hard to control, harmful to health, and draining. Xenophon, Plato, Aristotle, and the physician Hippocrates (fourth century BC) all look on it in this way."[13]

The suspicion and distrust towards sexuality in general and women in particular is nevertheless carried on through the Christian tradition. Ranke-Heinemann argues that although many consider the theologians of the Scholastic period, Thomas Aquinas and Albert the Great, as a turning

---

10. Ulloa, "Extending Ordained Ministry," 11.
11. Douglass, "Women and the Continental Reformation," 295–96.
12. Tertullian cited in Ruether, *Women-Church*, 138.
13. Ranke-Heinemann, *Eunuchs for the Kingdom*, 10.

point "in the tradition of Augustinian hatred of pleasure,"[14] it is abundantly clear from their writings that a deep mistrust of women exists. For example, in Albert's writings one reads:

> Woman is less qualified for moral behavior . . . women are inconstant and curious. When a woman has relations with a man, she would like, as much as possible, to be lying with another man at the same time. Woman knows nothing of fidelity . . . Woman is a misbegotten man and has a faulty and defective nature in comparison with his . . . one must be on one's guard with every woman, as if she were a poisonous snake and the horned devil.[15]

Out of such values grew the view that sexual intercourse should be engaged in, not for pleasure but solely for the procreation of children. Abstinence was admired and celibacy seen as a still higher state.

Schillebeeckx argues that the choice of celibacy cannot be invalidated simply by its origins in an antiquated anthropology and an ancient view of sexuality. Despite these origins he argues that one could today justifiably and legitimately undertake a celibate lifestyle, if it were freely chosen and if there was not a disdain for human sexuality in that choice.[16] He argues, "it must, however be said, that to lay open the history of the origin of a phenomenon does not imply anything either for or against its validity or truth."[17] Nevertheless, the points that I have made suggest that one must proceed in this discussion mindful of the origins of mandatory celibacy.

Many feminist scholars join Schillebeeckx in recommending that the Roman Catholic Church revise its theology of sexuality. Susan Ross proposes a feminist theology of sexuality drawing firstly upon the incarnation:

> God has come among humanity in fully human form, . . . all creation is graced, . . . God is mysteriously present in all things . . . God has come to dwell among us, in our flesh and blood, in our desires and joys. All that is created, including our sexuality, is good and is to be delighted in.[18]

Secondly, Ross argues that any theology of sexuality must be understood in the context of the Christian community. It is in community, in relationship

14. Ranke-Heinemann, *Eunuchs for the Kingdom*, 177.
15. Ranke-Heinemann, *Eunuchs for the Kingdom*, 178.
16. Schillebeeckx, *Church with a Human Face*, 245.
17. Schillebeeckx, *Church with a Human Face*, 245.
18. Ross, *Extravagant Affections*, 113–14.

with one another that human sexuality is nourished. The choice for celibacy is best understood in the context of mutually loving relationships within (and beyond) the Christian community. Following on from Ross's discussion, I suggest that decisions about the extent and nature of loving commitment need to be made in the context of human relationships and Christian community. For this reason, celibacy needs to be a matter of choice for the persons involved, and not a requirement laid down institutionally and out of the context of those relationships.

Catherine LaCugna remarks that many are no longer convinced that celibacy is desirable as a pre-condition for effective ministry: "Some would argue that mandatory male celibacy so predisposes the kinds of people who will apply that, far from authentically representing diversity within the church, it is bound to be unhealthy."[19] Although LaCugna is not suggesting that celibacy itself is unhealthy, the requirement of celibacy for all of the ordained is an unhealthy requirement. If the state of celibacy is not freely chosen, one's relationships with others can be hindered or adversely affected. The decision for celibacy is rightly made in the context of human relationship.

Is there, as Schillebeeckx suggests, any sense in which celibacy amongst ordained ministers can be seen as a sign? Janette Gray argues that celibacy can be a prophetic sign in which the celibate person shares in the suffering of the Creator and creation itself.[20] She argues however that human sexuality must not be repressed in this choice, but that celibacy be embodied in intimate human encounter.[21] Gray wrote in the context of women's religious communities, and for her the public nature of the commitment to celibacy was crucial: "A private and individualistic celibacy does not comply with the public nature of the vow."[22] If the requirement of celibacy for the ordained ministry were to become optional, as Schillebeeckx advocates, one could predict a dispensing of the public nature of this commitment. Celibacy could simply become a matter of personal choice. Unless those who chose to be celibate undertook a public vow to celibacy, is there any sense at all in which their celibacy is a prophetic sign? It is conceivable that a small proportion of ordained ministers might choose to make a public vow of celibacy. Such a vow would be best made in the context of a community

19. LaCugna, "Catholic Women as Ministers," 8.
20. Gray, *Neither Escaping nor Exploiting*, 60.
21. Gray, *Neither Escaping nor Exploiting*, 67.
22. Gray, *Neither Escaping nor Exploiting*, 69.

of loving support where celibacy does not deny, but seeks an alternative embodiment of human sexuality.

8

The Exclusion of Women from the Ordained Ministry

FEMINIST SCHOLARS ARE UNANIMOUS in their critique of the present exclusion of women from the ordained ministry of the Roman Catholic Church. I argue that this exclusion is damaging to the work of Christian ministry in the Roman Catholic Church. As Schillebeeckx notes,[1] many feminists no longer merely seek admission into patriarchal ministerial structures, but instead argue for a radical revisioning of the structure of ministry in the church. In their reconceptualization of the ministry of the church, feminist thinkers argue that the exclusion of women—either from the processes of reconceptualizing or from the ministry itself—cannot continue.

Schillebeeckx sympathizes with women and suggests that as long as they are "excluded from all the authorities which make decisions, there can be no question of the true liberation of women in and through the church,"[2] but he does not go so far as to see that the exclusion of women from decision-making and ministry in the church not only oppresses women but threatens the well-being of the church itself. Schillebeeckx seems to understand this exclusion of women as damaging to them, but not necessarily to the church. He does not allude to any damage to the church. Even in a later interview with Francesco Strazzari, published in 1993, Schillebeeckx merely commented that the church's failure to ordain women deprives

---

1. Schillebeeckx, *Church with a Human Face*, 239.
2. Schillebeeckx, *Church with a Human Face*, 239.

women of authority. What remained unsaid was that the church itself is deprived of the gifts of women. In this same interview, he claimed, "I am happy with the decision to confer the priesthood on women as well," which is different from lamenting the failure to ordain women. I am left wondering whether Schillebeeckx believes women's ordination to be a necessary move or merely an acceptable move.[3] Feminist scholarship, on the other hand, has argued that the church itself is less than whole while it continues to exclude women from the full ministry of the church.

Even thirty years ago, the closing address for the 1986 Washington Conference, "Ministry in Review," argued that the exclusion of women from the full ministry of the church is damaging to the church:

> The issue of women's ordination has become a symbol of the willingness or refusal of the Catholic Church to come to grips with the challenges presented by the contemporary society, with its emphasis on justice and the rights of people . . . Evading the problem will cause irreparable harm to the credibility of the Catholic Church.[4]

As Mary Hines argues, the problem is "not merely the exclusion of women from the church's ministerial structures but a deep-seated injustice deforming the very structures themselves."[5] The church itself is less than whole when its structure of ministry excludes women. Anne Carr argues for a model of church as "the sacrament of the incarnation of Christ into all of humankind,"[6] and for the ordination of women as well as men:

> [T]he church would fittingly express the mutuality of the human sexes and its service to both women and men by male and female ordination. If both men and women participated in all its ministries, it would be a fuller sacrament of the one priesthood of Christ in the whole people of God and of the apostolic witness of the message of Jesus to both men and women. It would be a clearer sacrament of the transformation of the priesthood from medieval clerical caste to the New Testament patterns of equality and mutuality that began to be reincorporated into church structures at Vatican Council II.[7]

---

3. Schillebeeckx, *I am a Happy Theologian*, 76–77.
4. Paul, "Plethora of Phoebes," 84.
5. Hines, "Community for Liberation," 170.
6. Carr, *Transforming Grace*, 36.
7. Carr, *Transforming Grace*, 36.

Part One—A Critique of the Traditional Theology

The symbolic power of women's exclusion from the ministry and from the decision-making processes of the church is profound and describes the undervalued status of women in the church. Anne Carr also suggests that the exclusion of women from the ordained ministry mirrors a broader situation in the church of an attitude of prejudice against women.[8]

Schillebeeckx offers no specific critique of the church's reasoning in excluding women from the full ministry and decision-making procedures of the church. What he does do, however, is advocate the need for change in the church. Arising from his historical overview of the form and practice of ministry, Schillebeeckx demonstrates clearly that the church's organization and theological understanding of ministry has changed down the centuries in response to changing political, social, and cultural factors. Change has always occurred in the life of the church, he argues, and ought to occur.[9] He also notes that in the ontological and sacerdotalist conception of ministry are the "pseudo-doctrinal hindrances" to women's ministry and to priestly marriage. He goes on to observe that "in ancient times, even in the Christian church, for once to put it bluntly, 'taboos' were associated with this sacralism: both feminine and sexual taboos."[10]

Feminist theologians and feminist movements such as Women's Ordination Conference (USA), Catholic Women's Ordination (UK), and Ordination of Catholic Women (Australia)[11] have thoroughly critiqued the church's teaching that excludes women from the ordained ministry, arriving at the conclusion that there is no theological or pastoral obstacle to the ordination of women.

In the Apostolic Letter of Pope John Paul II, *On Reserving Priestly Ordination to Men Alone,* John Paul lists his reasons for opposing the ordination of women:

> These reasons include: the example recorded in the Sacred Scriptures of Christ choosing his apostles only from among men; the

---

8. Carr, *Transforming Grace*, 45.
9. Schillebeeckx, *Church with a Human Face*, 2.
10. Schillebeeckx, *Ministry*, 98.

11. Ordination of Catholic Women was an Australia-wide organization. It was a group of women and men who advocated the ordination of women into a renewed priestly ministry in the Catholic Church. Dr. Marie Louise Uhr was the National Convener of this group since its foundation in 1993 until her untimely death in 2001. OCW continued its work until 2009, when it was deemed that it had achieved the purpose of mainstreaming the understanding of the importance of ordination for women within a renewed priestly ministry.

The Exclusion of Women from the Ordained Ministry

> constant practice of the Church, which has imitated Christ in choosing only men; and her living teaching authority which has consistently held that the exclusion of women from the priesthood is in accordance with God's plan for his Church.[12]

John Paul recalls the debate around women's ordination in the Anglican Communion and Pope Paul VI's rejection of it in the Catholic Church. John Paul notes that it was continued debate in Catholic circles that prompted the declaration *Inter Insigniores*, which again recalled the "fundamental reasons for this teaching."[13]

Each of the reasons given by the church over the years for excluding women from the full ministry of the church has been critiqued by feminist thinkers. Joanna Dewey, in the vein of Schüssler Fiorenza, questions whether in fact Jesus did name twelve men or any specific group to continue his ministry.[14] Schüssler Fiorenza argues convincingly that the historical existence of the twelve is not emphasized in the Q text,[15] but rather their eschatological symbolic function. The number twelve, she argues, "refers back to the ancient constitution of Israel consisting of twelve tribes and points forward to the eschatological restitution of Israel."[16] Furthermore, Schüssler Fiorenza argues, it seems that the twelve as a group were not replaced when they died, making it difficult to argue for the construct of "apostolic succession."[17]

It is difficult to ascertain that Jesus ever in fact envisaged a break with the synagogue, let alone intended the establishment of the church with an official ministry. Ann Graff raises this very question:

> At issue among scholars is whether Jesus had any intention of founding a church at all. The consensus is that he did not, nor did he design any institutional structures to create a church. The church is a response to Jesus, the Risen Christ, and the emerging institutional concerns we see in the gospel reflect the period in which they were written, after the Resurrection.[18]

---

12. John Paul II, *On Reserving Priestly Ordination*, 1.
13. John Paul II, *On Reserving Priestly Ordination*, 2.
14. Dewey, "Gospel of Mark," 479.
15. Q (quelle-source): A collection of sayings which seem to be the source of material common to Matthew and Luke, but not found in Mark.
16. Fiorenza, *Discipleship of Equals*, 109.
17. Fiorenza, *Discipleship of Equals*, 115.
18. Graff, "Infallibility," 10.

Part One—A Critique of the Traditional Theology

Such a line of argument does not necessarily dismiss the notion that Jesus is the founder of the church, for in making this latter claim, one ought to take into account the *whole* of the life, death, and resurrection of Jesus Christ. The church has its foundation after Christ's resurrection through the inspiration of Christ's Spirit, the Holy Spirit. From this time the earliest community begins to shape the structure and form of the ministry inspired in an ongoing way by a strong awareness of the presence of the Spirit of Christ amongst them.

John Paul has spoken of the "constant practice" of the church in choosing only men,[19] and yet as Schillebeeckx has clearly demonstrated, the form and practice of the ministry of the church has in fact been changing in response to changing political, social, and cultural factors. Miroslav Volf comments upon arguments that appeal to the unchangeable will of God and asks whether they are "serving rather to veil ideologically one's own interest in maintaining certain ecclesial structures."[20] As Volf demonstrates, there are *several* ecclesial models that can be retrieved from the early church tradition.

There are numerous examples of women involved in the ministry of the early church.[21] Though it has been the practice of the church to ordain only men, women have been involved in the ministry of the church since its inception. This occurred before the threefold ministry of bishops, priests, and deacons became fixed. However, as early as the close of the second century, women were restricted in their capacity to minister in the church.

It can also be demonstrated that the claim that it has been the constant practice of the church to ordain only men is inaccurate. Six women and a number of married men were ordained in the twentieth century in the Catholic Church in the former Czech Republic. This occurred in the late 1960s at a time when the church was under persecution from the Soviet Union and is now regarded by Vatican officials as invalid.[22] Ludmila Javorova was ordained by Bishop Felix Davidek, "a brilliant scholar, linguist and medical doctor who was consecrated with Vatican approval to serve in

---

19. John Paul II, *Reserving Priestly Ordination*, 3.

20. Volf, *After Our Likeness*, 22.

21. Some of these women include Euodia and Syntyche who worked "side by side" with Paul in the missionary movement (Phil 4:2–3); Phoebe, deacon (Rom 16:1); Junia and Prisca, fellow-workers with Paul (Rom 16:1); and Nympha, host of a house-church (Col 4:15), who had a role in opening up the Jesus movement.

22. Vlk, "Cardinal Confirms Catholic Woman's Secret Ordination," 768.

the underground church."[23] *OCW News* reports the occurrence, at a time when Javorova makes her story known to the western world:

> When a need for a sacramental ministry for women in prison emerged as a serious concern, it was clear that a male priesthood could not answer it. Davidek called a secret Synod composed of bishops, priests and laity to consider the ordination of women. After heated debate, the decision was made to proceed. On December 28, 1970, Davidek ordained the first woman priest, Ludmila Javorova, who served as Vicar General of the underground Diocese for 20 years.[24]

Despite such an extended period of service to the institutional church, the official Vatican line is that Javorova's ordination was invalid. It appears that the institutional church is prepared to go to considerable lengths to deny that women could ever be or have been ordained. Christine Gudorf comments upon the apparent importance to the papacy of the exclusion of women from the ordained ministry:

> Even threatened by the breakdown of the sacramental system itself because of a lack of priests, the papacy will not consider either ordaining women or allowing priests to marry . . . Maintaining the exclusion of women is even more important than providing communities with regular access to sacraments. This decision is all the more startling in view of the clerical insistence that sacramental life is real life—that the grace necessary to support Christian life is channeled primarily through the sacraments.[25]

In the light of the Czech experience during the Communist era, it seems that maintaining the exclusion of women from the full ministry of the church is also more important than acknowledging and affirming the twenty years of pastoral service already offered in the ordained ministry by Ludmila Javorova.

The church has argued that the exclusion of women from the full ministry of the church is God's plan.[26] What needs to be questioned in this line of argument is how and by whom God's will is discerned. It is the view of feminist scholars that discerning the will of God must take place in a wide context of reading the signs of the times, not merely in the inner world of

---

23. Ordination of Catholic Women, "Czech Woman Priest," 6.
24. Ordination of Catholic Women, "Czech Woman Priest," 6.
25. Gudorf, "Power to Create," 304.
26. John Paul II, *On Reserving Priestly Ordination*, 1.

the church but in the wider community. It must involve listening to the voices representative of all people, not merely a privileged few.

One of the arguments for excluding women from the ordained ministry that is put forward in *Inter Insigniores* is not carried forward into the more recent document, *On Reserving Priestly Ordination to Men Alone*. It is the argument that women cannot naturally resemble Christ who "was and remains a man."[27] Dennis Ferrara has argued that this argument relied on a misunderstanding of Aquinas's work. He explains that Aquinas understood the notion, *in persona Christi*, in an instrumental sense, in that the minister, despite his own otherness from Christ, allows Christ to work through him. The ordained minister is an instrument through whom Christ works, and does not, argues Ferrara, have to resemble Christ or "represent him visibly or externally."[28] If however the distinguishing feature of the ordained minister lies in their representation of the church (rather than Christ, who all the baptized are called to represent), the need for women to be amongst the ordained is even more compelling. As Kilmartin has claimed:

> Logically the representative role of priest seems to demand both male and female office bearers in the proper cultural context; for the priest represents the one Church, in which distinctions of race, class, and sex have been transcended, where all are measured by the one norm: faith in Christ.[29]

If ordained ministers are to represent the whole community of the baptized, it is essential that they be both male and female.

---

27. Sacred Congregation for the Clergy, *Inter Insigniores*, 12.
28. Ferrara, "Representation or Self-effacement?," 196.
29. Kilmartin, "Apostolic Office," 263.

PART TWO

Retrieving Relevant Understandings from the Tradition

THE FOLLOWING CHAPTERS TAKE up the task of historical retrieval, reviewing the tradition in order to reclaim or recover elements that may have been distorted, lost, or forgotten. It asks, "What is retrievable in the tradition that is freeing and redeeming for a renewed theology of ministry?"

The understandings and practices that will be considered include the egalitarian nature of the early Christian movement and the existence of women's leadership in that early Christian movement. The prophetic voices of women through the tradition are reviewed, along with the significance of baptism. The following pages argue for a retrieval of the significance of Christian baptism, along with a retrieval of the notion of *diakonia* or servanthood. And finally I propose that a retrieved understanding of the doctrine of the Trinity can be helpful in outlining a revisualized theology of the ordained ministry.

9

Retrieving the Egalitarian Nature of the Early Christian Movement

THE EARLIEST CHRISTIAN COMMUNITIES had an egalitarian strand in which the gifts of all the baptized people of God were valued and where women as well as men were involved in the ministry and leadership of the community. Both Schillebeeckx and Christian feminists argue that during the process of patriarchalization or institutionalization, the church became more formally organized and suppressed its egalitarian nature. Memory of this egalitarian strand must be retrieved as a valuable resource in the reconstruction of a theology of ordained ministry.

Schillebeeckx's theology of ministry is grounded in the notion that in the earliest Christian communities the power of the Spirit was foundational. Schillebeeckx argues that it is the Spirit of God, celebrated and recognized in the rite of baptism, that empowers and inspires the Christian community. The early Christian communities understood themselves as relatively egalitarian gatherings where there seemed at first to be no special roles or titles connected with ministry, leadership, or authority.[1] "Every member of the community had *de facto* authority in the community on the basis of his or her own inspiration by the Spirit."[2] The pre-Pauline baptismal formula of Galatians 3:27–29, Schillebeeckx argues, promotes an egalitarian view of

---

1. Schillebeeckx, *Church with a Human Face*, 59.
2. Schillebeeckx, *Church with a Human Face*, 37.

Part Two—Retrieving Relevant Understandings

the church in which discrimination on the basis of race, status, and sex are removed.³

Several Christian feminist theologians, including Elisabeth Schüssler Fiorenza, have analyzed the evidence from biblical and other texts and demonstrated that the Jesus movement of Palestine did indeed have a vision of itself as an egalitarian community in which structures of domination were not to be tolerated. Schüssler Fiorenza writes:

> Christianity has not been patriarchally determined from its very inception and has not been an integrated segment of its dominant patriarchal Jewish or Greco-Roman societies. If one asks which as yet unrealized emancipatory impulses in early Christianity are still historically accessible today in spite of the patriarchalizing tendencies of tradition and church, then one must adopt a reconstructive model that can bring to the surface the egalitarian impulses not only of the early Christian movements but also of their surrounding Jewish and Greco-Roman societies.⁴

She points to the Jewish settlement at Elephantine as an example of a society where women shared full equality with men, including serving in the military and contributing to the temple fund.⁵ Nevertheless these examples of egalitarianism did not represent the totality of Jewish life. Schüssler Fiorenza points to diverse Jewish renewal movements operating in the first century. One of these movements was the Jesus movement which came into conflict with the Pharisaic movement because it promised hope for *all* members, rather than emphasizing the holiness of the elect.⁶

Schüssler Fiorenza describes the Jesus movement as "a discipleship of equals"⁷ in which the full participation and leadership of women was encouraged. She delves behind the androcentric text of the Christian Scriptures to uncover the liberating vision that is encapsulated in the baptismal formula cited in Galatians 3:27–29. This formula, she argues, expressed the pre-Pauline missionary movement's "theology of the Spirit"⁸ a theology which brought about "new behavior . . . at least with respect to women who exercised leadership roles in the house churches and mission of the

---

3. Schillebeeckx, *Church with a Human Face*, 37–39.
4. Fiorenza, *Discipleship of Equals*, 174.
5. Fiorenza, *In Memory of Her*, 109.
6. Fiorenza, *In Memory of Her*, 120.
7. Fiorenza, *In Memory of Her*, 168.
8. Fiorenza, *In Memory of Her*, 209.

early Christian movement."⁹ Schüssler Fiorenza maintains that it has been the patriarchalization of the church and its sacred texts that has obscured the egalitarian nature of the early church and actually "manufactured the historical marginality of women." She suggests that the androcentric transmission of the early Christian tradition is in fact "not a reflection of the historical reality of women's leadership and participation in the early Christian movement."[10] It is by bringing a hermeneutic of suspicion to the androcentric texts and to the process of the canonization of the Scriptures that Schüssler Fiorenza uncovers the struggle concerning women's leadership in the church.[11] She argues that the process of patriarchalisation had to overcome an early egalitarian Christian theology in which the understanding of the community was one in which "there is no longer Jew or Greek, there is no longer slave or free, there is no longer male and female; for all of you are one in Christ Jesus"(Gal 3:28).

Karen Torjesen describes the adaptability of the early Jesus movement which enabled it to be more open to those traditionally oppressed: "In its earliest stages it is best understood as a social movement like any other. It was informal, often counter-cultural in tone, and was marked by a fluidity and flexibility that allowed women, slaves, and artisans to assume leadership roles."[12]

It is this strand of egalitarianism seen in the early Christian movement that needs to be remembered and retrieved, for it was in the struggle between patriarchal forces and the egalitarian strand that the place of the community in participating in the decision-making processes was forfeited. Schüssler Fiorenza describes this process with its shift in authority:

> (T)he shift which took place in the second century was not a shift from charismatic leadership to institutional consolidation, but from charismatic and communal authority to an authority vested in local officers, who—in time—absorb not only the teaching authority of the prophet and apostle but also the decision-making power of the community. This shift is, at the same time, a shift from alternating leadership accessible to all the baptized to patriarchal

---

9. Fiorenza, *In Memory of Her*, 209.
10. Fiorenza, *In Memory of Her*, 52.
11. Fiorenza, *In Memory of Her*, 55–56.
12. Torjesen, *When Women were Priests*, 11.

leadership restricted to male heads of households; it is a shift from house church to church as the 'household of God'.[13]

Schillebeeckx's description of the outcome of this process is remarkably similar. He claims that "the development of ministry in the early Christian churches was not so much as is sometimes claimed, a historical shift from charisma to institution but a shift from the charisma of many to a specialized charisma of just a few."[14]

Particular aspects of the early egalitarian Christian movement are in need of retrieval. They include the notion that authority and decision-making power ought to be vested in the baptized community and that the leadership of the community should be accessible to all of the baptized rather than to a small elite group. In the early Christian movement, the roles of teachers and prophets were not limited to the office-holders of the church but were located more broadly throughout the baptized community. These memories of an egalitarian structure need to be retained in the church because they are a critical resource necessary in the reconstruction of a theology of ministry.

I have asserted that the structure and form of the ministry of the church originally had distinct egalitarian strands. The memory of the historical process of patriarchalization by which the ministry became institutionalized is an important resource in the reconstruction of a theology of ordained ministry. The knowledge of a liberating vision at the heart and origin of Christianity is crucial in this work of revisioning. This egalitarian vision is revealed in the pre-Pauline baptismal formula, in which distinctions between Jew and Greek, between slave and free, and between male and female become unimportant in the light of Christ Jesus (Gal 3:28).

---

13. Fiorenza, *In Memory of Her*, 286–87.
14. Schillebeeckx, *Church with a Human Face*, 121.

10

Retrieving the Significance of Baptism for Ministry

I ARGUE THAT BAPTISM is the foundation of all ministry. However, baptism has been undervalued and has become an ambiguous symbol, particularly for women. The elevated status of the ordained clergy in the ministry of the contemporary Roman Catholic Church has acted to disempower the baptized people of God, but in fact the baptized have not only a role in the mission and ministry of the church but a responsibility to ensure that the ministry of the Christian church is always ongoing for the purpose of building up the Christian community.

Edward Schillebeeckx gives primacy and acknowledgement to the origin of all ministry in baptism. For Schillebeeckx, baptism is itself the ontological matrix and foundation for ordination. Baptism gives ministry its substance.[1] For some Christian theologians, ministry is, furthermore, the work of *all* the baptized. Maria Harris, for example, proposes this position:

> The claim to ministry as the work of all Christians is asserted around the globe . . . no longer is ministry seen as the exclusive work of one group . . . to put it more directly: if all in the church are to claim the work of ministry, the form and shape of the church must be examined, restructured and recreated, and the clergy-lay form may have to go.[2]

---

1. Schillebeeckx, *Church with a Human Face*, 205.
2. Harris, "Questioning Lay Ministry," 98.

Part Two—Retrieving Relevant Understandings

However, I agree with John Collins when he critiques this notion, arguing that not all baptized Christians are ministers.[3] Ministry is the public activity of a baptized follower of Jesus Christ that is carried out *on behalf of the Christian community*. This distinguishes ministry from other personal responses to the graciousness of God, which might not have a specifically public nature. Nevertheless, by virtue of their baptism, all Christians have a responsibility to ensure the uninterrupted ministry of the church and must be allowed to participate in the processes that will guarantee this ongoing work. In other words, not all of the baptized need be ministers themselves, but all of the baptized *do* share the responsibility of ensuring that the church's ministry is carried out.

For Schillebeeckx, it is clear that baptism in the Spirit is the foundation for an ecclesiology that is egalitarian and inclusive of both women and men.[4] Feminist theologians, however, have pointed out that because contemporary church structures are not egalitarian, baptism has become an ambiguous symbol for many women.[5] As a result the need has arisen to rehabilitate the meaning of the symbol of baptism.

The critique of present church structures and practices offered by feminist theologians highlights the tendency to grant status to the ordained and minimize the role of the baptized people of God, who at present neither have status nor any *significant* role in the decision-making procedures of the Roman Catholic Church. Those who are ordained are expected to take up a range of ecclesial functions, including pastoral work, sacramental activities, teaching, counseling, and parish or diocesan administration, whilst there is little recognition of the ministries of those who are not ordained.

I argue that the predominance of the ordained clergy in the ministry and mission of the contemporary church has acted to disempower the baptized people of God. This state of affairs has given the potentially powerful symbolism of baptism an ambivalent place in the lives of women. Schüssler Fiorenza argues that it is "patriarchal church structures which have marginalized and silenced women throughout the centuries and have denied us our baptismal right of being church."[6] Ruether argues that baptism should symbolize the overcoming of oppressive modes of human relationship and "the reunion with one's authentic potential for human life by entering into a

---

3. Collins, *Are All Christians Ministers?*, 1–3.
4. Schillebeeckx, *Church with a Human Face*, 39.
5. Procter-Smith, *In Her Own Rite*, 138–44.
6. Fiorenza, *Women*, xi.

community that represents redemptive human relationality."[7] Baptism, for Ruether, signifies a turning away from powers of oppression and a conscious disaffiliation from patriarchy. However, for women, baptism often marks an initiation into an institution that in fact perpetuates the powers of oppression rather than one which works to overcome them. Marjorie Procter-Smith has also acknowledged the ambivalence for women in baptism. The rite of baptism "serves to initiate both women and men into a patriarchal ecclesial structure and to maintain their identity with that structure even when it is oppressive."[8] She claims that the rites of baptism and Eucharist "as enacted in a patriarchal church, both construct and sustain the patriarchal structure of church."[9] She rightly recognized that the promises offered in baptism were not realized in the patriarchal church. The recollection of the early baptismal formula in the Pauline literature linked Christian baptism with the equality and dignity of all persons whatever their racial, social, or sexual status, and yet the rite of baptism has not accomplished the equality to which it is witness.[10]

Despite these claims, baptism is potentially powerful. Marjorie Procter-Smith points to the fact that baptism makes prophetic and priestly demands upon us that are empowering. She claims that those baptized, "the involuntary marginal—women—must express our baptismal right and responsibility as struggle for the transformation of the church, the world and ourselves."[11] Thus in feminist thinking, the need to retrieve the symbolism of baptism as an affirmation of the equality and dignity of all persons is made explicit. For feminist theologians, as for Edward Schillebeeckx, baptism is the foundation of Christian life, celebrating a person's initiation into that life. It is therefore the foundation of the church's ministry.

The implication of retrieving the foundational nature of baptism is that the baptized do not merely have a right to be engaged in the mission of the church (of which the ministry is a significant aspect), but a responsibility to do so which originates from their baptismal commission.

The Vatican II document, *Lumen Gentium*, although never specifically defining the role of the laity in the ministry of the Catholic Church, nevertheless quite emphatically states in several passages that all of the baptized

---

7. Ruether, *Woman-Church*, 77.
8. Procter-Smith, *In Her Own Rite*, 138.
9. Procter-Smith, *In Her Own Rite*, 138.
10. Procter-Smith, *In Her Own Rite*, 145.
11. Procter-Smith, *In Her Own Rite*, 148.

participate "in the saving mission of the Church."[12] *Lumen Gentium* presented a radical reorientation of the role of the people of God in the life of the church that had not before been evident in conciliar documents. In this document, the chapter "The People of God" is placed ahead of the discussion on the hierarchical structure of the church, and a precedence is given to the notion that all are called to be part of "this catholic unity of the People of God."[13] Baptism is the "door" by which people enter the church.[14] This renewed approach to the importance of baptism is a radical shift in understanding the role of all the baptized in the mission of the church. However, this new understanding, as Schillebeeckx has rightly argued, has not been given "any consistent institutional structures by the official church."[15]

Although renewed notions of the role of the baptized were given expression at the Second Vatican Council, a certain ambiguity remained as to the relationship between the ordained ministry and the whole of the baptized church. As I pointed out earlier, *Lumen Gentium* claimed that the ministerial priesthood did in fact differ in essence from the priesthood of all the faithful, but did not clearly describe this difference and neither did it spell out how the ministerial priesthood is related to the common priesthood of the baptized.[16] During the decades that followed Vatican II, the baptized faithful were increasingly involved in the ministry and the liturgical activity of the church, so that tensions arose within the church as to the proper role of both the ordained ministry and the baptized faithful in the ministerial work of the church. This tension was highlighted in the 1997 *Instruction on Certain Questions Regarding the Collaboration of the Non-ordained Faithful in the Sacred Ministry of Priest*. This instruction clearly seeks to "safeguard the nature and mission of sacred ministry and the vocation and *secular* character of the lay faithful . . . and correct abuses which have been brought to the attention of our Dicasteries."[17]

Whilst all are not necessarily called to carry out the formal or official ministry of the church, by virtue of their baptismal commission all Christians have the responsibility of ensuring that both the mission and ministry of the church is carried on. I have argued that, through the work of historic

12. Abbott, *Documents of Vatican II*, 59.
13. Abbott, *Documents of Vatican II*, 32.
14. Abbott, *Documents of Vatican II*, 32.
15. Schillebeeckx, *Church*, xiv.
16. Abbott, *Documents of Vatican II*, 27.
17. John Paul II, *Instruction on Certain Questions*, 4.

retrieval, both feminist scholars and Edward Schillebeeckx uncover the existence of an egalitarian strand in the earliest Christian communities in which baptism was regarded as the empowering source of inspiration A caveat to this finding for feminist scholars, however, is that in the institutional church of today, the symbol of baptism is ambiguous, especially for women, and its original meaning and power is also in need of retrieval.

11

Retrieving the Story of Women's Leadership in the Early Christian Movement

WOMEN WERE ENGAGED IN leadership roles in the early Christian movement and it is imperative that the memory of this be retrieved in order to demonstrate that the history of the church and its ministry is the history of both women and men. Scholars acknowledge that women were engaged in the leadership of the community even as early as the time of Jesus. Elizabeth Johnson seeks to "set the record straight"[1] in her retrieval of the role of Mary Magdalene as a powerful religious leader who made significant contributions to the ministry of Jesus. Johnson challenges the distorted stories of the tradition in which Magdalene is discredited and portrayed as a sexual transgressor.

> Like all lies, this robs her of the integrity of her own life. It cheats women out of the dangerous memory of her discipleship leaving them bereft of a key piece of history on which to build resistance to ecclesial male dominance, and it deprives the church as a whole of the prophetic power of the memory of women's leadership.[2]

According to the Gospels of Matthew and John, Mary Magdalene is the first to see the risen Christ and is presented in both accounts as a model

---

1. Johnson, *Friends of God*, 146.
2. Johnson, *Friends of God*, 146.

of discipleship. It is Mary Magdalene who has remained at the site of the crucifixion when the other disciples have fled; as the first witness of the resurrection, she is commissioned to convey this good news to the other disciples. This was a commission for a particular ministry, that of imparting the good news of Jesus's resurrection.

Schüssler Fiorenza points to the androcentric interpretation of the egalitarian primitive Christian tradition, particularly in its attempts to suppress the role of Mary Magdalene as the first witness of the resurrection. She notes the Lukan emphasis on Peter as the primary Easter witness and the apparent tension over this issue expounded in the Gospel of Thomas, the Gospel of Mary, and the gnostic text *Pistis Sophia*.[3] She concludes that this dispute over the resurrection witness of Mary Magdalene "shows, however, that Mary, like Peter had apostolic authority in some Christian communities even into the third and fourth centuries."[4]

Schillebeeckx and feminist scholars observe that both women and men were leaders of the earliest house communities. Christian communities gathered inside of the house and it was common for the leaders of these households to assume leadership within the early communities. Karen Torjesen remarks:

> First and second century Christians, familiar with the authority and leadership role of the female head of household, would have perceived women's leadership within the church as not only acceptable but natural. The early church's specific leadership functions posed no barriers to women, whose skills and experiences as managers amply prepared them to assume the duties of teaching, disciplining, nurturing, and administrating material resources.[5]

Rosemary Ruether and Eleanor McLaughlin argue that there is "no reason to assume that women were excluded from the leadership of the house churches or from presiding at worship."[6] Schüssler Fiorenza cites numerous examples of women as prominent leaders of the early church, some who were quite independent of Paul, others who existed before Paul, and others like Euodia and Syntyche who worked on an equal basis with Paul in the missionary movement.[7] She names Phoebe, Junia, Prisca, and Nympha as

---

3. Fiorenza, *In Memory of Her*, 50–51.
4. Fiorenza, *In Memory of Her*, 51.
5. Torjesen, *When Women Were Priests*, 82.
6. Ruether and McLaughlin, *Women of Spirit*, 33.
7. Fiorenza, *In Memory of Her*, 169.

Part Two—Retrieving Relevant Understandings

women who had a role in opening up the Jesus movement. Chloe, Prisca, and Phoebe are among the large number of active women in the Corinthian community. The Acts of the Apostles and the letters of Paul mention various ministries carried out by women as well as men, including deacon (Phoebe, *diakonos,* mentioned in Romans 16:1), coworkers (Prisca, mentioned in Romans 16:3), apostles (Junia, mentioned in Romans 16:7), disciples (Tabitha, mentioned in Acts 9:36) and prophets (the daughters of Philip, mentioned in Acts 21:9).[8] However, as Ford suggests, many translations of biblical texts describing women's leadership give weakened presentations of the role of women. The deacon Phoebe described in Romans 16:1–2, for example, is sometimes presented as "a mere helper or friend of many."[9] Karen Armstrong comments on this phenomenon: "This (the term, *diakonos*) is often translated "deaconess", as though there were already a separate and inferior order of women in the primitive Church. But this is simply a projection of subsequent practice back on to the Pauline era which knew of no distinction between 'deacon' and 'deaconess.'"[10]

Karen Jo Torjesen has made women's leadership of early communities the subject of her book, *When Women Were Priests.* She recalls the numerous examples of women who were leaders and accounts for their gradual subordination under the pervasive influence of Greco-Roman cultural views about gender. Importantly she points to the theological task that lies ahead for us today, which is one of "extricating the essential teachings of the Christian gospel from the patriarchal gender system in which it is embedded."[11] As Schillebeeckx, Schüssler Fiorenza, Ruether, McLaughlin, and Torjesen observe, Christian communities soon became patriarchal. Schüssler Fiorenza suggests that tensions soon arose in the early Christian missionary movements over egalitarian practices: "(T)he praxis of co-equal discipleship between slaves and masters, women and men, Jews and Greeks, Romans and barbarians, rich and poor, young and old brought the Christian community in tension with its socio-political environment."[12]

It was this tension engendered by the Christian vision of Galatians 3:28 which "became the occasion for introducing the Greco-Roman

---

8. Paul, "Plethora of Phoebes," 75–77.
9. Ford, "Women Leaders," 132.
10. Armstrong, *End of Silence,* 70.
11. Torjesen, *When Women Were Priests,* 268.
12. Fiorenza, *In Memory of Her,* 279.

patriarchal order into the house church."[13] As Schillebeeckx maintains, this occurred in order that non-Christians who would have been familiar with a strict hierarchical household would not be offended by Christians who lived as a discipleship of equals.[14] Christian communities were brought into the public realm and the role of women in the early church was gradually marginalized. As Schillebeeckx observes, by the time of the writing of the pastoral epistles the ministry of women is being curtailed:

> (F)rom now on women have to keep silent in services. This is more prescriptive than descriptive comment and it seems to presuppose what was earlier a different practice. Moreover, the instruction of women is now restricted to the teaching of women by women, which again indicates a different custom earlier (1 Timothy 2:11; Titus 2:3–5 are therefore not contradictory) The pastoral reason is always that non-Christians, who are familiar with a rigid and hierarchical household, must not be offended by the Christian life-style, which at these points differed from the cultural pattern in the empire.[15]

Ruether and McLaughlin conclude that the patriarchal house codes were a reaction to the leadership of women in the house churches, an assumption they also claim is supported by the text of Timothy 2, "where the injunctions that women should be submissive and not teach are given in the context of regulations for worship."[16]

As Camille-Paul points out, the attitude of Jesus towards women in all of the gospels is positive, for he never treats women as inferior.[17] Because Christ's message is good news for the poor, for the oppressed, and for the outcast it has always had a dangerous element that threatens to destabilize the power and status of the wealthy and politically and socially dominant. Perhaps it is little wonder that the early church very quickly assumed the patriarchal order of Greco-Roman society.

---

13. Fiorenza, *In Memory of Her*, 279.
14. Schillebeeckx, *Church with a Human Face*, 67.
15. Schillebeeckx, *Church with a Human Face*, 67.
16. Ruether and McLaughlin, *Women of Spirit*, 33.
17. Paul, "Plethora of Phoebes," 75.

12

Retrieving the Prophetic Voices of Women

DURING THE PROCESS OF institutionalizing the ministry of the church, the prophetic voices of women were suppressed. In his tracing of the growing institutionalization and clericalization of the Christian church, Schillebeeckx comments upon the historical appropriation of the prophetic role by the official church leadership: "The earlier authorities in prophecy and teaching are now swallowed up and incorporated into the authority of the one local bishop."[1] As early as the second century, Schillebeeckx suggests, the local leadership of the church had appropriated the roles of both prophets and teachers.[2] A consequence of this was the silencing of women and the consolidation of the sacral status of the ordained ministry. It is imperative then that the prophetic voice of women must be retrieved to provide vitality for the life of the contemporary church.

The combination of the containing of the prophetic voice within the offices of the church and the restricting of the official ministry of women has led through the centuries to the limiting of the prophetic voice of women in particular. This successful attempt at silencing women is illustrated by the paradigmatic story of the unnamed woman of Mark's Gospel. Both Elisabeth Schüssler Fiorenza and Marjorie Procter-Smith cite the example of the prophetic action of this woman who enacts the messianic anointing of Jesus, a liturgical act for which she is praised by him. He promises that her action will be recounted in her memory wherever the gospel is told.

---

1. Schillebeeckx, *Church with a Human Face*, 71.
2. Schillebeeckx, *Church with a Human Face*, 85.

Nevertheless, the name of this woman, who acts as both priest and prophet, is forgotten. As Procter-Smith notes, even the early Markan account of the story has either forgotten or suppressed her name.

> However, by the time the gospels were written down, the woman's name had already been forgotten... Our lectionaries largely ignore her, our liturgies of anointing do not remember her, our sanctoral cycles confuse her with Mary of Bethany or Mary Magdalene. The church has not kept Jesus' promise to this woman. The story of the forgotten woman and her liturgical act stands as a paradigm of the failure of the church in its liturgy not only to remember women and their liturgical-prophetic deeds, but also to respect women's memories. For the church not only failed to remember the woman's name; it also failed to remember the significance of the event.[3]

Procter-Smith suggests that we can view this story as a prototype of baptismal anointing in which the woman is the central actor. She is the presider, acting on behalf of the community, expressing the faith and love of the community in the Anointed One: "The memory of this woman's liturgical-prophetic act must be recovered, as a witness to the legitimacy and value of women's memory, women's prophecy and women's liturgical agency. We can only imagine what Christianity would look like if all baptismal anointings were performed in memory of her."[4]

There are other examples in the Christian Scriptures of the active ministry of women, but perhaps the story of the forgotten woman of the Markan Gospel is most poignant. Her act is prophetic, liturgical, and has a didactic function, and yet her actions are largely forgotten in the contemporary church.

Karen Torjesen recalls the significance of the prophets to the earliest Christian communities who acted as local leaders and were "accorded the honor of presiding over the eucharistic meal."[5] She remembers the prophetic witness of Elizabeth to the uniqueness of the child in Mary's womb and Mary's prophetic witness in the Magnificat.[6] Furthermore, she establishes that women prophets (such as Priscilla and Quintilla) and certain widows

---

3. Procter-Smith, *In Her Own Rite*, 38–39.
4. Procter-Smith, *In Her Own Rite*, 58.
5. Torjesen, *When Women Were Priests*, 26.
6. Torjesen, *When Women Were Priests*, 26.

were prominent in the early communities although by the second century their leadership and authority is challenged.[7]

Throughout history there are countless examples of women prophets who have considerable impact on the life of the Christian church. Many of the stories of these women have only come to light in recent years and in many cases some of the writings and sayings of these women have been downplayed or even suppressed. Although it is impossible to survey in detail the women prophets of the tradition, I will point to several key women prophets as examples, showing how the retrieval of their voice is critical for the life of the church today.

Although, as I mention above, it is as early as the second century that the prophetic leadership and authority of women is severely challenged in the Christian church, women appear strongly in both the gnostic and Montanist groups of the patristic period. It is difficult to comment upon the status of women within the prophetic Montanist movement since most of the surviving writing about Montanism is from the perspective of its opponents. Nevertheless it seems that Maximilla and Priscilla were leading Montanist prophets, along with Montanus himself. Rosemary Radford Ruether and Eleanor McLaughlin argue that they "were not just his companions and followers, but enjoyed equal spiritual gifts and leadership in the Montanist movement."[8] Alan Richardson writes of the fervor and challenge of Montanism and notes that "such movements have frequently put to shame the 'respectable' churches in many periods of history."[9]

The practices of groups such as the Montanists, challenging to the Christian church, are an example of "dangerous memory" which must be retrieved from the tradition and held as data for our contemporary reflection.

Sometimes it is difficult to determine the historical accuracy of prophetic stories of women as in the case of Brigid of Kildare, who is remembered as a spiritual and prophetic leader of fifth-century Ireland. While it is known that she founded several convent settlements in Ireland and a community of women at Kildare, legend also has it that she was ordained as a bishop. Mary Condren observes that some of the authors of literature about Brigid are "clearly embarrassed" by this story: "Interestingly, however, they do not attempt to deny it. Rather they claim that the bishop was 'intoxicated

---

7. Torjesen, *When Women Were Priests*, 38–46.
8. Ruether and McLaughlin, *Women of Spirit*, 41.
9. Richardson, *Dictionary of Christian Theology*, 223.

with the grace of God' when he ordained her and could not have known what he was doing."[10]

Whether or not it is accurate, it is significant that this story has survived transmission. Clearly, Brigid was regarded with honor and veneration in the Irish church and the story itself holds symbolic and prophetic power in its own right and for this reason requires retrieval.

Hildegard of Bingen, a prophet of the twelfth-century Rhineland region, was abbess and founder of a number of monasteries and her reputation as a prophet, teacher, and healer spread beyond the Rhineland. She is known today for her writings in theology, physiology, and health, and for her musical compositions. Her writings reflect a profound sense of relationship with the earth and deep respect for the integrity of the creation, often lacking in theological writing that came later. Hildegard was not afraid to decry corruption that she saw rife amongst the clergy at this time in history:

> (T)hey are plunderers of their congregations, through their avarice, devouring whatever they can: and with their offices they reduce us to poverty and indigence, contaminating both themselves and us . . . But now, let us tell them to fulfill the obligations of their priestly habit and office according to true religion, as the ancient Fathers established them, or depart from us and leave us what they have.[11]

Catherine of Siena, later made Doctor of the Church, was another woman who was a powerful voice in her time, a woman who ministered to many and sought to encourage people in their journey of faith. She corresponded with political figures, ambassadors, the papacy, and clergy, attempting to use her influence in the work of restoring peace in the church. Her best-known writing is *The Dialogue,* much of which arose from her mystical experiences and is characterized by passionate and sensual imagery. Her images of the Godhead, "You are a fire always burning but never consuming"[12] and of the Holy Spirit as a nursing mother "who nurses at the breast of divine charity"[13] convey something of her own desire of God. They are images that have not enjoyed prominence in the tradition.

---

10. Condren, *Serpent and Goddess,* 76.
11. Hildegard cited in Bowie and Davies, *Hildegard,* 105.
12. Catherine of Siena, *Dialogue,* 365.
13. Catherine of Siena, *Dialogue,* 292.

Part Two—Retrieving Relevant Understandings

The life and writings of the English prophet of the late fourteenth century, Julian of Norwich, are today being retrieved and valued. Austin Cooper who describes Julian's message as one of "immense hope," surmises that "it is little wonder that the dour age of the Reformation almost totally ignored her."[14] He argues that her theology of a God who is immanent found little support in the Age of Reason or the Enlightenment "when God was often portrayed as a remote and almost detached observer."[15] Julian's images of God as Mother, drawn from biblical allusions, need to be kept to the forefront, as they form part of a tradition which has been suppressed in the patriarchal church.

Therese of Lisieux, acknowledged as Doctor of the Church in October 1997, is one of the powerful prophetic women of the nineteenth century. Therese's desire to be a priest is often one of the lesser-known aspects of her life. "I want to be a priest; how lovingly I'd carry you in my hands when you came down from heaven at my call . . . dear Jesus, how am I to reconcile these conflicting ambitions, how am I to give substance to the dreams of one insignificant soul?"[16]

Despite the embarrassment and challenge that the prophetic voice brings to the official church, it is important that such writings be retrieved and held in the light of today as resources for our reflection upon the nature of the ministry of the church.

Mary McKillop, the first woman saint of Australia, has undoubtedly stood as a prophetic voice of the early Australian church, founding the Sisters of St. Joseph as a community committed to working with the poor and remaining committed to this vision through great difficulties. In the same Josephite order one century later, Irene McCormack wrote about the meaning of the Eucharist and ministry, less than a year before she was killed in Peru.

> I've given up trying to use the terms 'paraliturgy' or 'liturgy of the word' or any of the 'excuses' the official church uses to deny collaborative ministry its rightful place with women and married lay people. I used to try to do the 'right' thing and correct people when they came asking us to celebrate their 'Misas'. I've become

---

14. Cooper, *Julian of Norwich*, 8.
15. Cooper, *Julian of Norwich*, 8.
16. Thérèse of Lisieux, *Autobiography of a Saint*, 184

convinced that they are closer to the truth and were 'freeing' me to exercise Eucharistic ministry amongst them.[17]

The prophetic voices of women like Irene McCormack, who have spoken out about the ineffective state of the ministry of the church, are suppressed in the contemporary church. In a recent instruction from the Roman curia, *Certain Questions Regarding the Collaboration of the Non-Ordained Faithful in the Sacred Ministry of the Priest,* views and practices such as that expressed by McCormack are responded to with concern. "Though being born in very difficult and emergency situations and even initiated by those who sought to be genuinely helpful in the pastoral moment, certain practices have often been developed which have had very serious negative consequences and have caused the correct understanding of true ecclesial communion to be damaged."[18]

The prophetic voice of women is left in a vulnerable position in the face of suppression and reprimand from a powerful magisterium, and it is crucial that such dangerous memories as that of McCormack be remembered and incorporated into the memory of the official church. Maria Harris argues that prophecy must be reclaimed:

> They (the prophets) were the ones, and in our own day are the ones, who embody the pathos of God—God's grief over the human condition. They are the ones who will not keep silent, who continue to shout an agonizing "No" in the face of the evil surrounding us. They are the people, often, of non-receptivity to dogma, of resistance, and of dangerous memory.[19]

Mary Catherine Hilkert has argued that women's prophetic activity, especially through the work of preaching, is of profound importance in the church's ongoing work of illuminating the message of the gospel.

> (T)he very reality of women preaching, particularly in the liturgical context, shatters traditional stereotypes and suggests new models of church and ministry, a fuller version of humanity, both female and male, as created in the image of God, a more fundamental understanding of the image of Christ as located in baptism, and ultimately, new images of God.[20]

17. McCormack, "Do This in Memory," 33–35.
18. John Paul II, *Instruction on Certain Questions,* premise.
19. Harris, "Discipleship of Equals," 168.
20. Hilkert, *Naming Grace,* 164–65.

Part Two—Retrieving Relevant Understandings

There has been an inverse kind of recognition in that women from the community have been chastised by Vatican authorities for their outspokenness.[21] Nevertheless the recognizable existence of prophets in the church is a sign of hope, for they act to critique the tradition and to suggest new ways of being church and of viewing ordained ministry.

The prophets of the church, wherever they are located, serve as agents of critique, and collaboration with them can only be of benefit to the whole church. The exclusive appropriation of the prophetic role by the local leadership of the church since the second century has served to hinder the process of self-critique and has contributed to the silencing of women in the ministry of the church.

Schillebeeckx, while noting the appropriation of the prophetic and teaching roles into the office of the church, does not mention the silencing of the women prophets of the ancient church. For him the process of institutionalization is the narrowing of the ministerial gifts of the community into the office of the church. I have shown that feminist scholars go further to outline the implications for women in the growing institutionalizing of the church. A significant outcome of recovering and restoring the stories of women and women prophets to the history of Christianity is that the legitimization that has been granted to the patriarchal structures of both church and state is challenged and weakened.

---

21. During 1997, I and another woman, Vicki White, representing the Cabra Chapel community gave an address to the forum, "The Participation of Women In the Catholic Church in Australia" organized by the Australian Catholic Bishops Conference. The question we addressed was "What are the barriers to women's participation in the church?" Some months later Vatican officials contacted the Dominican Sisters in Adelaide voicing their disapproval of some of the contents of our address.

13

Retrieving the Notion of *Diakonia*

ALL BAPTIZED CHRISTIANS ARE called to the work of *diakonia,* which involves taking responsibility for one's own life and a radical orientation to others, the community, and the whole of creation. This work is foundational for Christian ministers. Nevertheless, the notion of servanthood, traditionally asked of the minister, can be problematic for women and for this reason needs rehabilitation.

For Edward Schillebeeckx, the notion of servant leadership clearly sits comfortably. He argues, "Authority lies in love which serves the church, a service; it is not social, let alone ontological, status."[1] Ministry for Schillebeeckx is above all a service to the community and one which "requires complete personal dedication from the one who is called through the community of God."[2] While his shift of emphasis from the status of the minister to the needs of the community is understandable and perhaps laudable, Schillebeeckx, unlike feminist scholars, does not draw attention to the misuse of the traditional notion of servanthood nor does he apparently see the need for any rehabilitation of the notion.

The notion of the ordained minister as "servant," despite having a long tradition in the Christian church, raises problems for many women who have worked selflessly and without question in subservient roles in homes, workplaces, and churches. Letty Russell explains this dilemma: "Women, like other oppressed groups, resent being identified with a role of servant

---

1. Schillebeeckx, *Church with a Human Face,* 204.
2. Schillebeeckx, *Church with a Human Face,* 234.

which has long been a symbol of their oppression in family, church, and society. It is simply not Good News to someone trying to break out of the 'servant class' to hear that God has called her to be a servant."[3]

Elisabeth Schüssler Fiorenza also rightly points out that a theology of service "has different implications for men and women, ordained and non-ordained, powerful and powerless."[4] Relegation to subservient roles has consistently been the experience of many women, and language that speaks of ministry as a service does not challenge this situation. Schüssler Fiorenza cites the common example whereby men often exercise ministry by virtue of ordination, whereas women's ministry is often not rewarded financially, socially, or professionally. She critiques the notion of ministry as service: "This theology does not seriously challenge the Church's structures of patriarchal hierarchy and the 'class' division between ordained and non-ordained ministries but exhorts those who have patriarchal clerical status and ecclesiastical powers to serve the laity and those in need."[5]

Lyn Rhodes observes that the understanding of the ordained ministry as servant leadership can also act to mystify and even mask clerical misuse of power. Ordained men are often given very powerful roles, such as bishops, and paradoxically called servants "while no servanthood role traditionally available to women carries any real power."[6] For this reason, the notion of ministry as a service is perhaps only useful where it brings a challenge to those who actually have power and privilege in the church or society. Marjorie Procter-Smith advocates this when she suggests that the image of the servant can act "as a corrective to clericalism," where those who already have power and authority in the church "need help in redefining the use of that power."[7]

The notion of the ordained ministry as servanthood is undoubtedly problematic, although the notion of *diakonia* is foundational in Christian thought. I suggest that it must be rehabilitated as a way of understanding Christian ministry. We should not use the notion of ministry as service, without drawing attention at the same time to its misuse. James and Evelyn Whitehead, in their discussion of leadership, do not use the term servant lightly. They observe that servant leadership has often been misinterpreted

3. Russell, "Women and Ministry," 48.
4. Fiorenza, "Waiting at Table," 85.
5. Fiorenza, "Waiting at Table," 85.
6. Rhodes, *Co-creating*, 81.
7. Procter-Smith, *In Her Own Rite*, 31.

in terms of privilege and status in the Christian community. "*Servant* too easily translates into slavery and servitude, while the service of leadership that Jesus demands arises not in a master/slave economy but among a community of disciples."[8]

James and Evelyn Whitehead both critique the traditional use of the term "servant" and describe the service that is required in Christian discipleship as oriented to the community and locating its authority in dependence upon God.[9]

Despite her misgivings about the notion of ministry as service, Letty Russell is one feminist thinker who works for a more accurate retrieval of the meaning of the term, *diakonia*, a term she claims Christians cannot avoid, so central is it to the gospel message. Through careful exegesis she demonstrates that even the Hebrew word *ezer* (helper), unlike its English interpretation, is not to be understood as a subordinate. Likewise, the service of Christ was not a form of subordination to others but rather a "free offering of self and an acceptance of service and love in return."[10] *Diakonia*, argues Russell, refers to a form of divine help rather than subordination or subjection to one other.[11] Service in the Scriptures is God's work into which women and men have throughout history been invited to participate: "Regardless of what the role of servant has come to mean in the history of the church and society, in the Bible it is clearly a role of privilege and responsibility to take part in God's work of service in the world."[12]

For Russell, the term *diakonia* is retrieved as the process of becoming more fully human. It involves, she argues, "taking responsibility before God on behalf of ourselves and our sisters and brothers in the work of Christ."[13] She cites Hans Küng's view that the opposite of *diakonia* is domination and misuse of power. "Or, to turn it around," she argues, "the opposite of domination is service or liberation."[14] Küng argues that power can be put to either good or evil ends. The church can abuse power by domination

---

8. Whitehead and Whitehead, *Promise of Partnership*, 103–4.
9. Whitehead and Whitehead, *Promise of Partnership*, 103–4.
10. Russell, "Women and Ministry," 54–55.
11. Russell, "Women and Ministry," 54–55.
12. Russell, "Women and Ministry," 55.
13. Russell, "Women and Ministry," 58.
14. Russell, "Women and Ministry," 57.

and by the maintenance of privileged positions or it can use power for the common good by service *(diakonia)*.[15]

Although traditional notions of ministry as servant leadership must be subjected to criticism, the essence of the Christian message invites one to radically orient oneself to others and to the whole of creation. Such a radical reorientation is in fact the Christian vocation of service. What has often been overlooked in a traditional notion of ministry is that *all* persons are called to such "service," not just those designated or ordained to the office of the church. It has been unusual in a traditional understanding of ministry to consider the minister as one who is a recipient as well as a giver of service. In fact there are countless examples of ministers who describe an experience of being enriched and gifted by the people they officially serve. Archbishop Oscar Romero once proclaimed that he had been converted to Christ by his own people.[16]

What can remain unnamed in ministerial situations is the rich offering of the materially poor, oppressed, sick, or imprisoned to the "servant minister," traditionally the one who gives. So often there is only a one-sided acknowledgement that the minister is giving to or serving the poor, when in fact one is also being served. Feminist thinkers critique notions of ministry in which mutuality amongst the community (ordained or non-ordained) of giving and receiving, hearing and speaking, teaching and learning is absent. They support an approach to ministry in which all members of the community both serve one another and receive the services of others.

This radical orientation and concern for creation must also involve oneself. There is no place in ministry for a negation of the self. This is not to be confused with the conscious choice to put aside one's own needs or desires for the service of another. Failing to acknowledge one's own needs and desires in ministry can have dangerous consequences, for these needs often surface unconsciously in a variety of ways. Connection to the self and the responsibility for one's own life must not be sacrificed in the name of service to others. Rather a radical concern for others flows out from deep connection to the self and the two nourish one another. I suggest that a useful model for imagining this way of relating is the triune God: three persons who "mutually inhere in one another" and whose love overflows to all of creation. I will explore this model more fully in the following chapter.

---

15. Küng, *Why Priests?* 27–28.
16. Romero cited in Gutierrez, *We Drink*, 32.

It should be noted that Elisabeth Schüssler Fiorenza is not convinced by many of the arguments for a retrieval of the notion of *diakonia*. She argues that "the notion of diakonia can be reclaimed by feminist theology solely as a critical category challenging those who have actual power and privilege in patriarchal Church and society."[17] She notes two strategies that feminist theologians have used in retrieving a New Testament notion of *diakonia* and is critical of both. The first understands *diakonia* as freely chosen service that is liberating. It is to be differentiated from servility and self-denial. However, Schüssler Fiorenza argues that this proposal does not take into account the fact that those who—in a patriarchal culture—are powerless and socialized into subservience and a life of servanthood, are *not* able to freely choose servanthood.[18] She has drawn attention to the ongoing misuse of power in which people, often women, are drawn into working under the domination of others. While I believe that Schüssler Fiorenza is right in claiming that many are not able to freely choose servanthood, I would argue that this does not mean we abandon the ideal of freely-chosen service, but rather that we continue to critique those very situations where people are socialized into servanthood as antithetical to the real meaning of *diakonia*.

The second strategy identified by Schüssler Fiorenza and utilized by Ruether focuses on redefining ministry as "power for" not "power over." Schüssler Fiorenza's dispute with this strategy is that it still gives credence to the patriarchal concept and institution of service theologically. The fact is, she argues, the patriarchal church "continues to exercise its ministry as power over."[19] In my view, Schüssler Fiorenza argues too rigidly that the notion of ministry as service is disempowering for women. I suggest a rehabilitated notion of service rather than reject the notion altogether because it has been misused. Not withstanding Schüssler Fiorenza's position, the notion of *diakonia* is foundational in Christian thought and must be rehabilitated as a way of understanding Christian ministry.

---

17. Fiorenza, *Waiting at Table*, 91.
18. Fiorenza, *Waiting at Table*, 89–92.
19. Fiorenza, *Waiting at Table*, 90.

14

Retrieving the Doctrine of the Trinity

IN PART TWO OF this book, I am arguing for the retrieval from the tradition of various understandings and practices of ministry: the egalitarian nature of the early Christian community, stories of women's leadership, the prophetic voice of women, the significance of baptism, and the notion of *diakonia*. I suggest now that the retrieval of all of these aspects of ministry can be supported and underpinned by a retrieval of the doctrine of the Trinity as a resource in understanding the ordained ministry.

Schillebeeckx moves part way towards this in his insistence on the recovery of the pneumatological dimension of ministry, as opposed to relying purely upon a christological basis for ministry. Catherine LaCugna and Elizabeth Johnson propose an understanding of the doctrine of the Trinity that describes the nature of God as essentially relational: as three diverse persons who mutually inhere as the one God. Certainly, a retrieved notion of the Trinity can provide a theological foundation for understanding the ministry of the church, as I will demonstrate.

Edward Schillebeeckx rightly insists that the ministry of the church be understood in ecclesial terms and that the ordained ministry be defined by its relationship to the community. He suggests that the view of ministry in the ancient Christian community was "pneuma-christological."[1] In *The Church with a Human Face*, Schillebeeckx discusses at some length

1. Schillebeeckx, *Church with a Human Face*, 206.

the move that took place within the early church away from an original pneuma-christological view of ministry "to a theology of ministry based directly on Christology."[2] He argues that the result of such an approach is "a theology of ministry with a suppressed and even concealed ecclesiology, with no foundation in the living reality of the community of believers who live by the Spirit."[3]

John Zizioulas has also noted the tendency—originating in scholasticism—of treating the subjects of ministry, ordination, and Christology in an autonomous fashion. He explains the effect of this view:

> This gives rise both to Christomonistic tendencies in understanding the person and ministry of Christ, and—what is more significant for us here—to great difficulties in relating the Church's ministry to that of Christ. Finally, and because of all this, ministry and ordination are not basically approached from the angle of the *concrete ecclesial community* but of the individual person (his "ontology" or his "function").[4]

Zizioulas rightly insists that the church's ministry can only be identified with that of Christ if "we let our Christology be conditioned pneumatologically."[5] Christ cannot be isolated from the Spirit in whose power he was able to minister. The God of the early Christians, argues Schillebeeckx, "was and is the God who did not leave Jesus in the lurch after his death, but made him the life-giving Spirit."[6] The ecclesiology of the early church had its source in the baptism in the Spirit and "the power of the Spirit was the basic conviction of this generation of Christians."[7]

Schillebeeckx thus justifiably critiques a theology of ministry that is based solely upon a Christology, where he claims "the danger of taking the Spirit into one's own hands becomes great."[8] He demonstrates the need for taking account of the pneumatological character of the ministry of the church and whilst this clearly provides a more developed ecclesiology, I argue that a theology of ordained ministry can be further clarified by explicitly proclaiming a *trinitarian* basis for ministry.

2. Schillebeeckx, *Church with a Human Face*, 206.
3. Schillebeeckx, *Church with a Human Face*, 206.
4. Zizioulas, *Being as Communion*, 209.
5. Zizioulas, *Being as Communion*, 210.
6. Schillebeeckx, *Church with a Human Face*, 34.
7. Schillebeeckx, *Church with a Human Face*, 37.
8. Schillebeeckx, *Church with a Human Face*, 206.

Part Two—Retrieving Relevant Understandings

The relationality of the triune God can provide a framework for defining ministry in terms of its relationship to the Christian community, and so retrieving its essentially ecclesial basis. Walter Kasper claimed that the two bases for ministry, the christological and the pneuma-christological, are in fact not unconnected and that both can be "mutually expanded within a trinitarian concept."[9]

Many theologians would agree with Schillebeeckx in his affirmation of the link between the Christian community and the ministry of the church. Mary Hines, for example, argues that this connection "must be restored if the present-day crisis in ministry is to be resolved."[10] She reminds her readers that the church is the place where the Spirit dwells and where ministry is given birth. It is my contention that the retrieval of a relational trinitarian theology can provide a solid foundation for a theology of ministry which links ministry with community. The paradigm of the triune God provides a way of apprehending the interrelatedness of the community and the ministry.

In recent centuries the paradigm of the Trinity has been separated from the actual experiences of people's lives: experiences that originally gave rise to the doctrine. This has meant that the symbol of the Trinity has become irrelevant to many and as Elizabeth Johnson argues, it now appears merely "as esoteric doctrine that one could well do without."[11] Schillebeeckx himself touches upon this irrelevance when he responds to Strazzari:

> I confess the Trinity, but these speculations on relations between the three persons say nothing to me. The mystery cannot be rationalized, and when people like St. Augustine, St. Bonaventura, St. Thomas, Rahner, etc., do rationalize it, the result is that these trinitarian theologies do not say anything about the mystery of God that is of any use to spirituality. They are pure rationalization; perhaps very interesting, but cold.[12]

Catherine LaCugna addresses the question of why trinitarian theology has become irrelevant and formulates a restored understanding of the Trinity based on the economy of salvation with radical implications for Christian life. She notes that historically we have focused upon the ontological

---

9. Kasper, "Ministry in the Church," 185–95.
10. Hines, "Praxis of the Kingdom," 129.
11. Johnson, *She Who Is*, 192.
12. Schillebeeckx, *I am a Happy Theologian*, 54.

relationship between the Father, Son, and Holy Spirit rather than what God does in salvation history and she rightly argues that "the mystery of God and the mystery of salvation are inseparable."[13] One cannot divorce the inner life of God from what God does in history. In fact the inner life of God is unknowable. What we do know of God has been revealed to us in human history. LaCugna comments: "the question of God's being and God's self-communication in Christ and the Spirit are intrinsically connected."[14]

When the understanding of the triune God as radically related to all human life and indeed the whole creation is retrieved, then it is reasonable to suggest that the life of the church and of the ordained ministry ought, as much as is humanly possible, to embody or manifest the life of the Trinity. In their retrieved relational understandings of the doctrine of the Trinity, Elizabeth Johnson and Catherine LaCugna both propose an understanding that the triune God is by nature self-communicating or self-expressive, seeking to reveal and give of God-self.[15] LaCugna claims that "trinitarian theology is par excellence a theology of relationship."[16] Johnson expresses a similar opinion: "Speaking about the Trinity expresses belief in one God who is not a solitary God but a communion in love marked by overflowing life."[17]

Schillebeeckx's critique of traditional theologies of the Trinity claims that rational speculation about the nature of God does not impinge on our lives. However, the telling point that both LaCugna and Johnson make is that the very nature of the triune God *is* to impinge on our lives. God can do nothing other than this, for God is by nature relational.

In her book, *God for Us*, Catherine LaCugna suggests that the doctrine of the Trinity, a particularly Christian way of speaking about God, "summarizes what it means to participate in the life of God through Jesus Christ in the Spirit."[18] God, the mystery of three persons in communion, is "essentially relational, ecstatic, fecund, alive as passionate love."[19] The communion between the three persons of the Trinity not only entails an equality, a mutuality, and a reciprocity amongst the three but it overflows

---

13. LaCugna, *God for Us*, 4.
14. LaCugna, *God for Us*, 6.
15. Fox, "Trinity as Transforming Symbol," 273–94.
16. Fox, "Trinity as Transforming Symbol," 243.
17. Johnson, *She Who Is*, 222.
18. LaCugna, *God for Us*, 1.
19. LaCugna, *God for Us*, 1.

Part Two—Retrieving Relevant Understandings

to include humanity as its beloved partner.[20] God exists as three persons in mutual and loving relationship and is oriented in relationship to the whole of creation. The triune God, suggests LaCugna, "exists as diverse persons united in a communion of freedom, love and knowledge."[21] It is because God is triune, she argues, that the life of God does not belong to God alone, but is essentially related to our life and has bearing on our relationships to one another.

LaCugna, drawing from Rahner's notion that God is by nature self-communicating, rightly insists that the doctrine of the Trinity is the affirmation of God's intimate communion with us. Elizabeth Johnson, in her assertion that the relatedness of God is revealed in the triune God, claims: "At the heart of holy mystery is not monarchy but community; not an absolute ruler, but a three-fold *koinonia*."[22] Although LaCugna, like Johnson, does not hold to the notion of God as an absolute ruler, she does not so easily dismiss the concept of the monarchy of God. "Monarchy comes from *mone arche*, one origin, one principle, one rule,"[23] LaCugna reminds her readers. The one origin or cause (the Father), generates the Son and the Spirit, communicating and sharing the *arche* of God without subordination.[24]

The doctrine of the Trinity describes God as three unique persons mutually indwelling in one another. In this relationship, neither the uniqueness of the three persons nor their particularity diminishes the unity of God. In fact, quite conversely, the profound richness of the mystery of communion is revealed and enhanced by the uniqueness and the diversity of the three persons. Within this community of love, there is mutuality, equality, and a deep respect for difference. The notion that the three persons of the Trinity mutually inhere in one another and yet differ from one another is affirmed in classical theology. LaCugna cites the eighth-century theologian John Damascene who used the term *perichoresis* to describe this relationship. She argues, "*perichoresis* means being-in-one-another, permeation without confusion."[25] The perichoretic relatedness of the three persons at the same moment values the oneness of God and the diversity of

---

20. LaCugna, *God for Us*, 274.
21. LaCugna, *God for Us*, 243.
22. Johnson, *She Who Is*, 216.
23. LaCugna, *God for Us*, 389.
24. LaCugna, *God for Us*, 389–90.
25. LaCugna, *God for Us*, 270–71.

Retrieving the Doctrine of the Trinity

God, because the three persons though inhering in one another do not lose their distinctiveness.

Miroslav Volf, in his discussion of perichoresis, notes both the mutual inherence of the Father and the Son in one another, and yet their distinction from one another. He argues: "This is why both statements can be made: 'Father and Son are in one another' and 'Christians are in *them*' ("in *us*"—plural!: John 17:21)."[26] Volf argues that to think consistently in trinitarian terms means to avoid any dichotomy between universalization and pluralization. The one God *is* a communion of three divine persons. The unity and the multiplicity of God are equiprimal and he rightly argues that it is important that the tension between these two facets is not resolved.[27]

Catherine LaCugna and others have also affirmed that the trinitarian model of God is not hierarchical. Amongst the three persons in God there is no supremacy of one over the other. LaCugna comments at some length on Patricia Wilson-Kastner's reading of the Trinity, in which Wilson-Kastner advocates the notion that interrelationship is constitutive of divine reality. Wilson-Kastner states: "Put very simply, if one images God as three persons, it encourages one to focus on interrelationship as the core of divine reality, rather than on a single personal reality, almost always imaged as male."[28]

LaCugna argues that Wilson-Kastner's perspective of the Trinity rightly suggests that patterns of hierarchy are "ungodly, (and) antithetical to trinitarian life."[29] LaCugna's understanding of the Trinity nevertheless differs from that of Wilson-Kastner, in that she insists upon beginning her reflections in the economy of salvation, where all persons "divine as well as human,"[30] are in communion. LaCugna argues that the view that an egalitarian human community is an icon of God's relational life is more convincingly supported by returning to the economy of salvation. Her critique of hierarchy is soundly based in the *arche* (rule) of God. Her explication of the Trinity, grounded in the revelation of God in Jesus Christ through the power of the Spirit reveals the *arche* of God as "the shared rule of equal persons in communion, not domination by some persons over other

---

26. Volf, *After Our Likeness*, 209.
27. Volf, *After Our Likeness*, 193.
28. Wilson-Kastner, *Faith, Feminism and Christ*, 122.
29. LaCugna, *God for Us*, 273.
30. LaCugna, *God for Us*, 274.

persons."³¹ God's rule, LaCugna advocates, is "the antithesis of tyrannical, solitary or patriarchal rule"³² and is the foundation for a mutual, equal, and non-hierarchical social order.

Elizabeth Johnson argues that there is no one pattern of authority in the life of God indicated in the gospels, even though in the tradition a pattern of dominance and subordination has been suggested "between Father from whom all proceed and Son and Spirit who do the proceeding."³³ She argues that what is evident in the gospels is a variety of ways of relating. Thus although the Father sends and commissions the Son in Luke's Gospel, in John's Gospel the Son reveals and glorifies the Father. In John's Gospel the Son sends the Spirit and yet in Luke it is the Spirit who comes upon Mary to give birth to the Son. Drawing on this variety of texts, Johnson suggests: "There is no one pattern set in stone, in literal fashion, but all these texts attempt to give expression to the one mystery of self-communicating love approaching the world to heal, redeem, and liberate."³⁴

Although Johnson argues that there is no one pattern of authority or power evident amongst the three persons of the Trinity, I suggest that the locus of authority that is revealed by the three persons of the Trinity is surely the *koinonia* of the triune God. Johnson is right to suggest that power does not reside in any one person of the Trinity, for as LaCugna has argued, the rule or principle of God is communicated to and thus shared by more than one person.³⁵ The very authority and monarchy of the Father has been communicated and shared in the *koinonia* of God. The Unoriginate Source of all communicates and shares the divine *arche* and authority to reign. As LaCugna argues, God cannot be "Father" in isolation.³⁶ Authority is located not in any one person of the Trinity, because Father, Son and Spirit are co-equal, but in the *koinonia* of God, which owing to the economy of salvation, necessarily extends beyond the inner life of God.

Miroslav Volf critiques the traditional notion that there are hierarchical relations between the persons of the Trinity. "Even if the Father is the source of the deity and accordingly sends the Son and the Spirit,"³⁷ he

31. LaCugna, *God for Us*, 394.
32. LaCugna, *God for Us*, 398.
33. Johnson, "Trinity," 307.
34. Johnson, "Trinity," 308.
35. LaCugna, *God for Us*, 390.
36. LaCugna, *God for Us*, 390.
37. Volf, *After Our Likeness*, 217.

Retrieving the Doctrine of the Trinity

argues, there is a fundamental equality amongst the divine persons "in their mutual determination and their mutual interpenetration."[38]

> (H)e (the Father) also gives everything to the Son and glorifies him, just as the Son also glorifies the Father and gives the reign over to the Father (Matthew 28:18; John 13:31–32: John 16:14; John 17:1; 1 Corinthians 15:24). Moreover, within a community of perfect love between persons who share all the divine attributes, a notion of hierarchy and subordination is inconceivable. Within *relations* between the divine persons, the Father is for that reason not the one over against the others, nor "the First", but rather the *one among the others*.[39]

Volf's view of the structure of trinitarian relations leads him to critique what he describes as Ratzinger's "pyramidal dominance of the one"[40] and John Zizioulas's "hierarchical bipolarity between the one and the many."[41] For Volf, the structure of trinitarian relations is characterized by a "polycentric and symmetrical reciprocity of the many."[42]

Catherine LaCugna argues decisively that we cannot speak of God without speaking of all creation. The mutual love that inheres in the midst of God is not contained but overflows. God is truly a *God for* us.[43] Because the mutual love of the three persons of the Trinity is overflowing beyond God-self to all creation, it is in the very nature of God to invite the beloved people of God into participation in God's life. Elizabeth Johnson argues similarly that "if as the icon suggests, the holy mystery of God is not an isolated, absolute ruler but an incomprehensible, threefold *koinonia*, then the symbol of the Trinity functions to call forth loving relationships in the community and in the world."[44] In her earlier publication, *She Who Is*, Johnson argued similarly that the triune symbol "lays the foundation for a liberated society of equal brothers and sisters, critiques patterns of unjust

---

38. Volf, *After Our Likeness*, 217.
39. Volf, *After Our Likeness*, 217.
40. Volf, *After Our Likeness*, 217.
41. Volf, *After Our Likeness*, 217.
42. Volf, *After Our Likeness*, 217.
43. The notion of God being essentially "for us" is foundational to LaCugna's work and expounded upon throughout her book, aptly titled *God for Us*. It is a turn of phrase and a notion that has also been widely discussed by Edward Schillebeeckx.
44. Johnson, "Trinity," 300.

Part Two—Retrieving Relevant Understandings

domination, and offers a source of inspiration for change."[45] The life of God both embodies and calls forth loving relationships and enables the human community itself to embody and call forth loving relationships.

I have shown that the doctrine of the Trinity reveals God who is essentially relational, who is three persons united in radical communion, who is non-hierarchical, whose authority is grounded in the *koinonia* of the three persons, whose mutual love between three persons overflows to all creation, and who calls forth loving relationships in the Christian community. It is these qualities, revealed by the triune God, that provide a framework for revisioning a theology of ordained ministry.

---

45. Johnson, "Trinity," 300.

PART THREE

Revisioning the Ordained Ministry

IN THIS FINAL SECTION I will propose a vision of the ordained ministry, developed in part out of a critique of present church structures and more traditional theologies of ministry and by retrieving essential elements of the tradition. A retrieved understanding of the Trinity will be used as a key resource in a reconstructed theology of the ordained ministry.

As I demonstrated earlier, the main focus of Schillebeeckx's writing has been to review the data of history and to critique more traditional theologies and practices of ministry, rather than to reconstruct a theology of the ordained ministry. Feminist scholars have also reflected on their negative experience of oppressive church structures and on their experiences of what is liberating and nourishing. I have used these reflections as a resource for reconstructing a theology of the ordained ministry, a task that extends beyond the essential work of critique and retrieval to a work that is oriented to the future and the needs of the future church.

15

The Symbol of the Trinity

The Foundation for a Reconstructed Theology of the Ordained Ministry

IN THE PREVIOUS CHAPTER I put forward an understanding of the Trinity that describes a God who is "for us." God, who is three diverse persons united in radical communion, is inherently relational. LaCugna too, argues that the symbol of the Trinity ought to be a basis for ecclesial life:

> [W]e may ask whether our institutions, rituals and administrative practices foster elitism, discrimination, competition, or any of several archisms, or whether the church is run like God's household: a domain of inclusiveness, interdependence, and co-operation, structured according to the model of *perichoresis* among persons.[1]

She suggests that although the symbol of the Trinity does not prescribe precise forms or structures for the church it does nevertheless provide a critical principle against which we can evaluate present practices. She argues that the church is called to be "an icon of the Trinity" inasmuch as its members "exist together 'perichoretically', in mutual giving and receiving, without separateness, or subordination, or division."[2] Church leadership, she suggests, is to be "rooted in the ministry of service, not of lordship."[3]

---

1. LaCugna, *God for Us*, 402.
2. LaCugna, *God for Us*, 402.
3. LaCugna, *God for Us*, 402.

Part Three—Revisioning The Ordained Ministry

Persuaded by LaCugna's suggestion that the doctrine of the Trinity has practical application, I propose that the triune God is the agent and inspiration for right relationship in the human community. Since the Christian community is invited to participate in the life of the triune God, the symbol of Trinity is the *means* towards the shaping of the ministry of the church. The triune God, who is essentially relational, is the animation and life which underpins the very work of ministry. The foundation, therefore, for all ministry is in a baptism into the life of the triune God. We are reminded of this in the command of Jesus: "Go therefore and make disciples of all nations, baptizing them in the name of the Father and of the Son and of the Holy Spirit" (Matt 28:19). Baptism invites all who are baptized into participation in the prophetic, pastoral, and political mission of the church. This mission, which is inspired by the Spirit of God, was revealed in the person of Jesus, "prophet, priest and king," and reveals something of the very nature of God.

Lumen Gentium affirms this call to the baptized people of God to participate in Christ's mission:

> These faithful are by baptism made one Body with Christ and are established among the people of God. They are in their own way made sharers in the priestly, prophetic, and kingly functions of Christ. They carry out their own part in the mission of the whole Christian people with respect to the Church and the world.[4]

I suggest that the very life of the triune God calls forth the "priestly, prophetic and kingly" functions of the church's mission, which I shall call the pastoral, prophetic, and political dimensions of discipleship. Because all of the baptized are called to Christian discipleship, these dimensions are also foundational for ministry, which is grounded in baptism. Thus although all the baptized are not necessarily called to ministry, all ministers are called to fulfill the pastoral, political, and prophetic dimensions of discipleship. Before moving on, I will enlarge upon these three dimensions of discipleship.

The pastoral dimension of mission and ministry is concerned with nourishing and upholding right relationships amongst the people of God and between the people and God. The essential relationality of the triune God is embodied in the pastoral dimension of mission and ministry, which has as its goal a commitment to the relationality of the community and wider society. All of the pastoral work of the church, acts of healing,

---

4. *Lumen Gentium* 31, in Abbott, *Documents of Vatican II*, 57.

teaching, preaching, or reconciling, is grounded in the commitment to relationality. Acts of healing, teaching, preaching, or reconciling cannot be carried out without the underlying premise that relationships between people matter and that the connections between people and the whole of creation are worth nurturing. Nurturing the connectedness or relationality of the community is the essence of the pastoral dimension of mission and ministry. James and Evelyn Whitehead describe this work further:

> To nurture commitment means to strengthen the emotional and intellectual bonds that hold the group together. Leaders nurture commitment by keeping the facts of our interdependence before us. Effective leaders reinforce the conviction that we need one another . . . Effective leaders show us the benefits of belonging.[5]

Ideally, relationships between the people of the Christian community are based upon the people's interdependence and manifest the mutual and interdependent relationality of the three persons of the Trinity.

It is helpful to view the political dimension of mission and ministry in the light of the mutuality and equality that is inherent in the life of the triune God and sought by the Christian community. I have argued that in God there is no hierarchy, but a mutuality and equality between the three diverse persons. By recognizing the giftedness of all the baptized and enhancing the mutual empowerment of all persons, the mission and ministry of the church manifest the mutuality and equality of God. "Good leaders release other people's power . . . Effective leaders invite people to recognize their own gifts and offer these to the common task . . . effective leaders do not just regulate resources; they make *more* of the group's resources."[6]

The doctrine of the Trinity affirms that authority is located in the *koinonia* of the three persons who are united in mutuality and equality. Neither power nor authority resides solely in any one person of the Trinity, for the rule of God is communicated from the Unoriginate Source and shared by more than one person.[7] Father, Son, and Spirit are coequal. The authority of God rests in the *koinonia* of God, which owing to the economy of salvation necessarily extends beyond the inner life of God.

The mission and ministry of the church is prophetic in that it is oriented to the future, and calls forth from the community a similar mutual and just way of being. This dimension of mission and ministry is revealed

---

5. Whitehead and Whitehead, *Promise of Partnership*, 105.
6. Whitehead and Whitehead, *Promise of Partnership*, 106–7.
7. LaCugna, *God for Us*, 390.

Part Three—Revisioning The Ordained Ministry

in the nature of the triune God, who does not remain apart from creation but invites all persons to participate in the very life of the Trinity.

I acknowledge the limits of the analogy of the Trinity. The doctrine of the Trinity is a model, or as LaCugna suggests, "an icon" which points to the mystery of God but is not *in itself* the mystery of God. She suggests "[t]he doctrine of the Trinity is more like a signpost pointing beyond itself to the God who dwells in light inaccessible."[8] Miroslav Volf makes the same point, arguing, "our notions of the triune God are not the triune God."[9] Our understanding of God is drawn from human experience through history and although this experience is often inspired by and closely connected to God, as such it can never completely describe the fullness of God. A further limitation for the analogy of the Trinity lies in the limitations of the human community. As human persons, in our brokenness, we will not in fact be fully able to model our structures upon God. Volf reminds us that we are "a sojourning church," moving towards the eschatological fullness of our vocation, but not yet at that reality.[10] Given the limitations he sees to the analogy, Volf is not deterred from his argument that the relations between "the many in the church must reflect the mutual love of the divine persons."[11] The mutual love of the divine persons is not only reflected but also manifested or embodied in the church. LaCugna claims "[t]he nature of the church should manifest the nature of God."[12] This is a significant point of difference between Volf and LaCugna. Volf's language suggests mutuality as an "intra-divine" quality to be imitated by the church. As LaCugna convincingly argues however, the perichoretic nature of God necessarily extends beyond the inner life of God and embraces all of creation. The church will not merely reflect the trinitarian life of God but because it is caught up in the life of God, the church will live or give expression to that life.[13]

The pastoral, political, and prophetic dimensions of discipleship underpin the mission of the church to which all of the baptized are called, and therefore also underpins the ministry of the church to which some are called. I suggest that the ministry of the church and the ordained ministry

8. LaCugna, *God for Us*, 321.
9. Volf, *After Our Likeness*, 198.
10. Volf, *After Our Likeness*, 199.
11. Volf, *After Our Likeness*, 195.
12. LaCugna, *God for Us*, 403.
13. LaCugna, *God for Us*, 276.

in particular ought to embody or give expression to the life of the triune God who is essentially relational, who exists as three diverse persons in one God, and whose nature is to work in collaboration with humanity and all of creation. This means that the ministry too must be essentially relational. Secondly, ministry ought to manifest the non-hierarchical nature of God in its very structure. Thirdly, ministry must give expression to both the unity and diversity of God, by being diverse in nature but united in its purpose of building the Christian community. Finally ministry must be prophetic, calling forth right relationship from all persons.

16

Ordained Ministry: An Expression of the God who is Three Persons in Mutual Relationship

THE MINISTRY OF THE church, which is essentially related to the Christian community, ought to manifest the mutual and equal relations that are manifest in the triune God. More specifically, the peoples of the Christian community are related to one another, and the ordained ministers of the church have a distinctive relationship with the Christian community and the world. The commitment to this essential relationality in the Christian and wider community is the pastoral dimension of ministry.

The symbol of the Trinity, which describes the relatedness of God, provides a foundation for understanding these relationships. The nature of the Trinity, three unique persons in one God, can underpin and animate a way of relating in the Christian community which acknowledges the uniqueness of all persons, the equality of all and the diversity of both the Christian and wider community. The nature of the triune God affirms that right relationships within the Christian community and with the wider world ought to be highly valued and nurtured. The nature of the Trinity underpins the notion that the ministry of the church ought to be grounded in the *koinonia* of the Christian community, that is, in the essential relatedness or the bond of discipleship in the community.

How are the diverse aspects of the Christian community related to one another? How is the ministry of the church related to the Christian community and more specifically how are *ordained* ministers related to the Christian community and to each other? These questions can be examined with the insight that the triune God is essentially a God of mutual and just relationship and calls the ministry of God's church also to manifest mutual and just relationship.

THE RELATIONSHIP BETWEEN THE PEOPLE OF GOD

The Christian community is fundamentally united, although in practical terms this is not always clear. Nevertheless it is an essential tenet of the Christian faith that we are one: "For in the one Spirit we were all baptized into one body—Jews or Greeks, slaves or free—and we were all made to drink of one Spirit"(1 Cor 12:13). The baptized members of the Christian community are therefore fundamentally connected to one another, as are branches of a vine (John 15:1–11). In fact, as Christians configured to Christ through our baptism, we are called to represent Christ to one another and more widely to others outside of the Christian community.

In spite of the divisions within the church that damage the cause of the gospel, the Christian community, in so far as it is in Christ, is radically one. Christians are called to a genuine community in which right relationship is embodied.

The very nature of God is revealed to us through the person of Jesus Christ in the power of the Holy Spirit. All baptized Christians are therefore called to participate in God's life by standing *in persona Christi,* acting as Christ to others, through the inspiration of the Spirit. Traditionally the Roman Catholic Church has attributed this representational function solely to the ordained minister, when it properly belongs to all of the baptized. LaCugna explains the meaning of *in persona Christi* in practical terms:

> Living trinitarian faith means living as Jesus Christ lived, *in persona Christi:* preaching the gospel; relying totally on God; offering healing and reconciliation; rejecting laws, customs, conventions that place persons beneath rules; resisting temptation; praying constantly; eating with modern-day lepers and other outcasts; embracing the enemy and the sinner; dying for the sake of the gospel if it is God's will.[1]

---

1. LaCugna, *God for Us,* 400–401.

Part Three—Revisioning The Ordained Ministry

This is the way of relationship to which all baptized Christians are called and it is embodied in human life through the inspiration of the Spirit. It is the way of Christian discipleship. For this reason, this fundamental mode of relating, that of standing *in persona Christi* to one another, is also fundamental to all ministry. All ministry is grounded in this call of baptism.

The *public ministry* of the church has a particular relationship to the Christian community. It is in the context of the Christian community that ministry arises. Ministry, activity that builds up and nourishes the people of God, is born within the community and is carried out on behalf of the community by ministers who may or may not be ordained. Many recognized ministries of the church are not conferred with ordination, but all ministries arise within the Christian community, are inspired by the Spirit of God, and have as their purpose the building up and nourishment of the Christian community. In this way, all ministry ought to be seen as intrinsically related to the community in which it arises.

THE RELATIONSHIP BETWEEN THE ORDAINED MINISTRY AND THE CHRISTIAN COMMUNITY

The ordained ministry as a particular dimension of the church's ministry has a distinct and essential relationship to the Christian community. Schillebeeckx has noted that discussions about the meaning and function of the ordained minister traditionally have been far too centered upon the ontological character of the ordained person and too little concerned with the relationship of that person with the Christian community.[2] John Zizioulas claims that "there is a fundamental interdependence between the ministry and the concrete community of the church."[3] Ministry is not to be understood, he suggests, in terms of what it gives or does to the ordained, but rather *in terms of the relationship* into which it places the ordained:

> In the light of the *koinonia* of the Holy Spirit, ordination relates the ordained man [sic] so profoundly and so existentially to the community that in his new state after ordination he cannot be any longer, as a minister, conceived in himself. In this state, existence is determined by *communion* which qualifies and defines both "ontology" and "function".[4]

2. Schillebeeckx, *Church with a Human Face*, 155–56.
3. Zizioulas, *Being as Communion*, 212.
4. Zizioulas, *Being as Communion*, 226.

I suggest that the essential relatedness of the three persons of the Trinity is a paradigm that affirms the importance of the relationship between the ordained minister and the community. Attention is thus shifted away from the question of the ontological character of the minister to the relationship between the minister and the community. Although Zizioulas's view of ordination could be seen to undervalue the individual personhood of the minister, it does demonstrate the essential nature of the relationship between the community and the person ordained. Ordination itself has no meaning outside of the Christian community.

Ordination is bestowed upon those ministers of the church who have the distinctive symbolic task of maintaining the unity or connectedness and the diversity of the Christian church. This is ideally accomplished when the ordained minister arises from and is affirmed as a leader in the local community and is therefore able to represent the diverse local community to the universal church and to represent the universal church to the local community. In other words, ordained ministers stand *in persona ecclesiae*: their distinctive role is that of representing the one, holy, catholic and apostolic church. The distinctive task that they are to accomplish is to maintain and consolidate both the unity and diversity of the church.

The ordained ministry is more than the assignation of leadership by a community upon a person. All ministry is inspired by the Spirit of Christ and originates in Christ but the capacity for the ordained ministry in particular is discerned as a gift in a person *by the community in conjunction with the wider church*. The wider church affirms leadership by ordaining a person. Ordination thus signifies a particular relationship between the ordained minister and the Christian community. This relationship has been brought about through the work of the triune God, but it is ritualized, formalized, and celebrated through the rite of ordination. Ordination enables the ordained one to represent the universal church to the local community. It is not specific, practical duties that distinguish the ordained ministry from the rest of the ministry, but rather the symbolic role of representational leadership that acts to maintain and consolidate both the unity and diversity of the Christian church. The ordained ministry symbolically demonstrates the connection that is established and maintained between all Christian communities who, despite great diversity, belong to the one, holy, catholic, and apostolic church. The church is one and the ministry of the church is one.

Part Three—Revisioning The Ordained Ministry

THE RELATIONSHIP BETWEEN THE THREEFOLD MINISTRIES

It is fitting at this point to describe how the threefold ministries of the church are related to one another. Previously I maintained that the ordained ministry ought not to be hierarchically ordered such that those higher in the hierarchy are understood to have power over those below them. The mutuality and equality of the three persons of the Trinity invites the manifestation of a non-hierarchical way of relating amongst ordained ministers. The episcopacy, presbyterate, and the diaconate can be viewed as three unique ministries that, rather than form a hierarchy, offer a way of organizing the ministerial structure of the church.

I suggest that the locus of authority in the church ought not to be lodged in one particular person or role, but rather be grounded in the partnership of all the baptized: in the *koinonia* of the Christian community. This is a natural expression of trinitarian faith, because in the Trinity, as LaCugna points out, the One Origin shares and communicates the *arche* of God without subordination by generating the Son and the Spirit and by reaching out in ecstatic love to all of creation.[5]

The distinctive role of the ordained ministry is the symbolic function of representational leadership that acts to maintain and consolidate both the unity and diversity of the Christian church. The bishops in particular, as representatives of the universal church and of their local dioceses, act to consolidate and show forth the unity and diversity of the church throughout the world.

A second and particular function of each bishop is that of oversight, a function, I believe, which ought not to be understood either as a dominating or authoritarian role but rather as holding together and protecting the diversity of local communities. This task involves the nurturing of links between local communities and between the universal church and local communities. It is through the position of the episcopacy that the unity of local communities is made manifest. This role is not without tension, since the very diversity of communities can give rise to variations in values, religious practices, and theological understandings. Cultural practices which may have a long history in a local community may need to be woven into the practices of the wider church in the local context.[6] The church must

---

5. LaCugna, *God for Us*, 390–92.

6. This interweaving of local religious customs and universal liturgical practices

preserve the essence of the apostolic tradition but continually engage in necessarily critical inquiry, which is the work of theology. It is the bishop who bears a particular responsibility for the preservation of the apostolic tradition, and yet must be open to and encouraging of critical reflection upon the tradition, and to the ongoing revelation of God in the world. This unresolvable tension must be held by the bishops as part of the responsibility of *episkope* or oversight.

Presbyters, as ordained ministers and representatives of the universal church and of their local communities, also act to consolidate and show forth the unity and diversity of the church. They are intrinsically and traditionally related to their local bishop and cooperate in the work of the bishop. The situation which has arisen today where presbyters travel across the world to work in other communities which are supposedly without ministers ought to be viewed as an anomaly. I suggest that the norm is that presbyters serve the local community in which their ministry arose, thus maintaining the link between presbyter and the local bishop. Local communities, as Schillebeeckx has argued, if they are open to the Spirit of God, will give birth to ministry. I suggest that it has been the requirement of the western Latin church—that this ministry be confined to celibate males—that has given rise to a perceived paucity of ministers.

I propose that leadership in the local community ought to be shared and collaborative rather than lodged in the hands of one person. Nevertheless, it will be expedient for one or more persons to coordinate such leadership. This is a suitable function for presbyters.

Deacons, like the presbyter and bishop, are representatives of the universal church and their local communities, and act to consolidate and show forth the unity and diversity of the church. In the present hierarchical ordering of the threefold ministry, the diaconate is often understood as a stepping stone on the way to the presbyterate. The original meaning of the diaconate is lost in this contemporary interpretation. As I suggested previously, there is a need to retrieve the earliest meaning of *diakonia* as a radical

---

contributes to the diversity of communities. For example, some indigenous North American Catholic communities have incorporated the traditional practice of smudging into the eucharistic celebration, a practice which enhances and furthers the notion of blessing present in the Catholic tradition. Other communities have local concerns: for example, the people living at the base of the volcano, Mt. Vesuvius, call upon the locally revered St. Gennaro for protection from harm when the volcano erupts. Universalizing such local customs would be absurd, and yet the significance of local custom for the local community deserves protection.

Part Three—Revisioning The Ordained Ministry

orientation to God's work which involves a deep concern for the sacredness of one's own life, for all others, and for the whole of creation. Although the work of *diakonia* is the call to each baptized Christian, the diaconate can be understood as a particular crystallization of that work. As a representative of the church community and the wider church, the deacon focuses upon ministerial works that are both aspects of the call to *diakonia* and responses to the needs of the local community. The deacon in this way cooperates with the work of the bishop and is intrinsically related to the local bishop.

The presbyter too, like all of the baptized, is called to the work of *diakonia*. However in the contemporary church, the presbyter, unlike the deacon, is able to preside at the eucharistic table. As I have suggested already, there has been a narrowing of focus in the presbyterate around the Eucharist. What ought to be emphasized as distinguishing the presbyter from the deacon is not the capacity to preside at the Eucharist but the responsibility for the coordination of leadership of the local community. As representative of the local community and of the wider church, the presbyter's ministry is primarily that of leadership of the local community. This leadership ought to be in collaboration with other ministers and non-ordained members of the baptized community. It follows of course that presbyters, by virtue of their leadership, also preside at the Eucharist, but this need not to be seen as the presbyter's primary role.

The ordained ministry, sanctioned and affirmed by the one church, thus serves to connect and unify the peoples, communities, and nations that are represented by each minister. The distinguishing feature of the ordained ministry is its role of representing the one, holy, catholic, and apostolic church, a role that maintains and consolidates both the unity and diversity of the church. Having established this symbolic function, the practical functions of ministry are many and cannot be left to ordained ministers alone, but rather to those who are called and gifted in pastoral work.

To summarize, the ministry of the church ought to give expression to the relationality of the triune God. I have shown how the people of God are intrinsically related to one another, how the ministry is related to the community, and how the threefold ministries of bishop, priest, and deacon are related to one another. All of these relationships ought to live out the equal and mutual relationship that exists between the three persons of the Trinity.

17

Ordained Ministry: Manifesting the Mutual and Non-hierarchical Nature of God

THE MINISTRY OF THE church ought to be collaborative and non-hierarchical. The calls of many theologians for collaborative and mutual ministry are substantiated by referring both to the non-hierarchical nature of the triune God and to the significance of Christian baptism.

Johnson, LaCugna, and Volf argue that the Trinity is non-hierarchical.[1] The icon of the Trinity, in fact critiques ways of relating that give elevated status to any role in the community, since its very life honors the equality, mutuality, and distinctiveness of three persons united in the one God. In the Trinity there is no basis for domination or "power over" others. Trinitarian faith suggests that the ministry of the church ought to be collaborative rather than based in the authority and responsibility of the few. The mutuality and equality of the persons of the Trinity affirms the claim that the relationships amongst the office-holders of the church and between the office-holders and the rest of the baptized ought to be collegial, collaborative, and offer mutual service to one another. In a collaborative ministry, the interaction between ministers and the community is highly valued and responsibility is shared.

---

1. Johnson, *She Who Is*, 194–97; LaCugna, *God for Us*, 270–78; Volf, *After Our Likeness*, 214–20.

Part Three—Revisioning The Ordained Ministry

The insights of feminist theologians offer a variety of models of understanding the ministry of the church that are essentially non-hierarchical and collaborative. Lynn Rhodes, for example, illuminates the nature of ministry by using the images of friendship and solidarity. In Rhodes's thinking, the church itself is a community of friends, who are interdependent, mutually caring, and accountable to one another.

> [F]riendship suggests both the emotional intimacy we need and the mutuality, nurture, trust, and accountability that we value. The most powerful and best friendships we have give us insight into love that implies reciprocity and an authority of selfhood that neither demands the other's acquiescence nor makes the self subservient. It does not deny uniqueness, nor does it require hierarchy in order to be functional.[2]

Rhodes's model for ministry is consonant with the paradigm of the perichoretic love of the triune God. No persons have particular power or authority over another, but rather respond to one another mutually. Rhodes's view of ministry affirms the often neglected aspect of ministry, that of the authority of selfhood. The minister does not and ought not to live solely for others. If acknowledgement is not given to the needs and value of one's self, it becomes impossible to live for others. True regard for another's personhood can only be given in conjunction with attention to one's self. We deny the authority of selfhood in the ministry at our peril, for the demands of the self, if ignored, will arise, albeit in unconscious and destructive ways.

A collaborative form of ministry influences the ways in which those in the community relate to one another. Carol Lakey Hess, like LaCugna and Johnson, notes that the Christian understanding of the triune God is "inherently relational and conversational,"[3] and for this reason she argues that an appropriate way of relating in Christian communities is by conversation that is characterized by deep connection, cooperation, and mutuality. She advocates conversation that is empathetic, non-judgmental, receptive, passionate, honest, and self-disclosing.[4] If ministry is to be truly collaborative, it is important that there is a mutuality in exchanges between those who minister and those who receive ministrations. It is important that ministers are able to receive ministrations from others. All of the baptized, whether ordained or not, may at different times be engaged in both the giving and

---

2. Rhodes, *Co-creating*, 123.
3. Hess, "Education as an Art," 65.
4. Hess, "Education as an Art," 65.

receiving of ministrations. This means that there may not be strict divisions between those who learn and those who teach, or those who serve and those who are served.

Maria Harris documents a shift in thinking in terms of education within the church, from a process of "officials indoctrinating children to obey the church" to "the whole community educating the whole community to minister to and in the world."[5] Harris stresses that the responsibility for ministry belongs to the whole community and the whole community ought to be open to learning. I concur with Harris that the responsibility for ministry belongs to the whole community, but I believe that this does not necessitate the whole community carrying out the public work of ministry. Using Harris's example of the task of education, it is clear that not all of the baptized will have gifts as educators, and some will be more gifted than others. Our task as a Christian community is to be open to the gifts of the baptized and not assume that the office-holders of the church are the sole educators.

Ann O'Hara Graff, in her discussion on hierarchical ministerial structures where leadership and pastoral care is lodged in one person of elevated status, proposes a mutual ministry. "The women I know want a church of mutual ministries in which care for one another and support of outreach to work for love and justice are based on common discernment of the gospel in our local situations. Thus ministry is constitutive of the life of the community, never separate from it."[6] She suggests the need to work for a church in which people relate with mutuality and reciprocity: "They look toward a community in which people sustain one another, forgive and help one another, nourish and celebrate each other's gifts. Co-responsibility is the key. Ministry is exercised from within the community to facilitate and empower the members, to enhance the well-being of each, and to work for the welfare of the whole."[7]

Graff's model of church and ministry in which responsibility for sustenance or pastoral care is not lodged in one person, but is rather shared amongst the community, is consonant with the mutuality and reciprocity inhering in the nature of the triune God.

---

5. Harris, "Discipleship of Equals," 154.
6. Graff, "Women in Roman Catholic Ministry," 226.
7. Graff, "Women in Roman Catholic Ministry," 218.

Part Three—Revisioning The Ordained Ministry

Rosemary Ruether's proposal for a non-hierarchical ministry envisioned a community of "enablers."[8] Since no one person has all the skills to satisfy the needs of the community, she rightly argued that the community itself must look among its ranks for those with gifts. These people will be empowered to use their talents and use them to develop the talents of others.

Marga Bührig summarizes some of the contributions of women in proposing alternative models of church:

> A growing number of women within and outside the churches are no longer content to accept office in an unchanged and patriarchally structured Church. They are looking for new models (e.g., the 'Church of Women') summed up in expressions such as 'participatory', 'communicative', 'partnership', 'non-hierarchical' and 'reciprocity of ministries'.[9]

Each of the terms Bührig uses suggest an equality and mutuality between the baptized members of the community. All of the baptized members of the Christian community, although differing in gifts and functions, are called to participate in the life of the community, to nurture their connection with one another, and to collaborate with one another towards the building up of the Christian community.

The positions on ministry that I have outlined call for non-hierarchical ministerial structures and advocate collaborative and mutual ministry. These views are consonant with the paradigm of the triune God that describes three persons existing in mutual and equal relationship. The paradigm of the triune God can offer a theological underpinning for the call for non-hierarchical and collaborative ministry. The positions on ministry that I have outlined are also consonant with the retrieved notion of *diakonia* that I have described earlier: that the work of *diakonia* does not involve the domination of others but rather the taking of responsibility before God in the work of Christ. In this understanding, the people of God are interdependent and take up a responsibility towards themselves and towards others in a radical concern for the whole of creation. The way of relationship between the people of the Christian community and between the community and its ministers ought to embody that between the three diverse persons of the Trinity: it must value mutuality, equality, and loving collaboration.

---

8. Ruether, *Women-Church*, 89–90.
9. Bührig, "Role of Women," 97.

Ordained Ministry: Manifesting the Nature of God

Elizabeth Johnson has argued that the Christian Scriptures do not advocate any one pattern of authority in the life of God.[10] My view is that whilst the Scriptures do not consistently advocate the lodging of authority in any *one* of the three persons of the Trinity, authority can be located in the *koinonia* of the triune God. The triune God has authority for us as Christians. It makes no sense to speak of the authority of the Father or any one person of the Trinity in isolation from the other two persons. The authority of the triune God can only be understood in the context of the *unity* of the three diverse persons. God has authority as a triune God, three persons bonded in equal and mutual love. It is in this bond of unity, the *koinonia* of God, that the authority of God is lodged. In like manner, within the Christian community authority ought to be invested in the *koinonia* of the Christian community. This suggests that in collaborative styles of ministry, authority ought not to be located in one person, over and against others, but ought rather be invested in the bonds of relationship between the baptized faithful. This is not to say that there is no place for leadership. It is to suggest that the bishop's role of oversight and leadership ought not to be an authoritarian one, but one which involves collaboration with the people of God and a respect for the authority of discernment processes which involve the representation of views from the whole of the believing community.

In her revisioned model of church, Letty Russell locates authority in community: "Authority is exercised *in* community and not *over* community and tends to reinforce ideas of co-operation, with contributions from a wide diversity of persons enriching the whole."[11]

For Russell, leadership in the Christian community is best exercised by standing with the community in solidarity with those who are most marginal. Authority is not domination over others but is exercised in community and in partnership. Russell's point of view can be strengthened by using the paradigm of the triune God as a theological basis for her claim.[12] That is, the authority of God rests in the *koinonia* of the three persons of the Trinity, affirming that for the Christian community, authority is best invested not in any one person but in the *koinonia* of the community.

Paul Hypher, too, rightly argues that authority in the church ought to based upon the *koinonia* of the community.

---

10. Johnson, *She Who Is*, 191–223.
11. Russell, *Household of Freedom*, 34–35.
12. Russell, *Church in the Round*, 67–73.

Part Three—Revisioning The Ordained Ministry

> One of the major issues in the rethinking of ordained ministry must be that of authority. At present the call to collaborative partnership of lay people and clergy is blighted by a poor exercise of authority by the clergy and by poor decision making processes . . . the gospels suggest that it is equally illegitimate for the Church to claim that it or its ministers are an autocracy. What then is the legitimate exercise of authority in the church? It is the exercise of authority which is based on the nature and essence of the divine gift of koinonia.[13]

The icon of the Trinity consolidates the argument that the locus of authority ought to be grounded in the *koinonia* of the Christian community. If authority is to be discerned within the community, structures must be in place that enable the diverse voices of the people of God to be heard, considered in the light of the whole community and in the light of the tradition, and for decisions and actions to be taken. Feminist theologies support the notion that authority should be invested in the *koinonia* of the community, and they critique situations where power is wielded *over* people rather than exercised *with* people. Feminist theologies embrace a radically relational world view which demands a struggling toward mutual and just relationships, and they critique situations where power is used to dominate or subjugate others.

Earlier I pointed to the need to retrieve the significance of baptism from the tradition. When the baptismal commitment of the people of God is properly recognized, there will be a movement towards more collaborative ministry. Kathleen O'Brien and Margaret Early have recognized this phenomenon: "There has been a movement from more hierarchical authority structures to participative leading, in part due to the need and recognition of the diversity of gifts and abilities of all the baptized, and also because of the increased presence of women in leadership roles."[14]

The church, argued LaCugna, can be an icon of the Trinity, where it embodies the mutual love of the triune God, where there is mutual giving and receiving, and unity in love amid diversity.[15] Ordained ministers can manifest this mutual love where they are both conscious of their own role in the church and also value and nourish the vocation of all baptized Christians. Ministers manifest the life of God when they both give love,

---

13. Hypher, "Future Models of Ordained Ministry," 104–5.
14. O'Brien and Early, "Women," 158.
15. LaCugna, *God for Us*, 403.

support, and nourishment to others and receive love, when they both teach and encourage others and are the recipients of others' teaching and encouragement. Whilst there is a common responsibility for the life of the church amongst all of the baptized people, the task of the ordained ministry can be seen as one of facilitating or enabling the work of Christian discipleship. Volf rightly argues that the ordained person is not to do everything, but to "animate all the members of the church to engage their pluriform charismatic activities, and then to co-ordinate these activities."[16] This mutuality in relationship must extend beyond the church to the whole of the human community, such that the ministry of the church is both conscious of its own calling but open to the voices of those outside of the Christian community.

Feminist thinkers tend to favor shared leadership that is based upon the diversity of gifts in the community. This is in contrast to situations where leadership is placed in the hands of one person. The mutuality and equality of the persons of the Trinity affirms the claim that the relationships amongst the office-holders of the church ought to be collegial. Authority ought never to reside in one person. There have been times in recent history in the Roman Catholic Church when the position of the Bishop of Rome has assumed undue prominence at the expense of the mutual and collegial relationship that ought to exist amongst all of the bishops of the church. Schillebeeckx describes the Petrine function, which he sees as that of providing unity, as "one ministerial service among many other ministries in the church."[17] Schillebeeckx rightly relativizes the Petrine function, which nevertheless fulfills a function in the contemporary Roman Catholic Church. The Bishop of Rome could ideally serve to act in collaboration with the college of bishops in order to maintain and consolidate the unity of the church by holding together the diversity of the churches of the nations of the world. In this role, the Bishop of Rome together with all bishops could facilitate communication amongst the baptized people of God and coordinate the collaboration of the people of God in the mission and ministry of the church. There must be a deep respect for the diversity of the church as well as its unity, so that cultural differences which affect liturgical and religious practices are not merely tolerated but appreciated. There must also be a deep respect for the collegiality of the church. Miroslav Volf, following the thought of Heribert Mühlen, argued that each of the offices of

16. Volf, *After Our Likeness*, 230.
17. Schillebeeckx, *Church*, 199.

the church, including the papacy, ought to be exercised collegially.[18] Basing his ecclesiology upon the symbol of the triune God, Volf argued that one person simply cannot represent the unity of the triune God: "If one starts from the trinitarian model I have suggested, then the structure of ecclesial unity cannot be conceived by way of the one, be it the pope, the patriarch, or the bishop. Every ecclesial unity held together by a mon-archy, by a 'one-(man!)-rule,' is monistic and thus also un-trinitarian."[19]

I do, however, perceive a role for the bishop: one that involves the representation of the universal church to the local diocese and also the representation of that local diocese to the universal church. Volf is right to say that the unity of the church cannot be entirely represented in one person. Nevertheless, one person, i.e., the bishop, can be a focus for that unity. Each bishop is a focus for the unity of the whole church and the *task* of the bishop is to consolidate and maintain that unity.

Using Catherine LaCugna's notion that the monarchy or *arche* of God is self-communicated and shared by more than one person, a firm case can be made for supporting the argument that each of the ministerial offices ought to be exercised collegially. "Quite clearly the doctrine of God has vast political implications, and it matters greatly whether the doctrine of God is trinitarian or unitarian . . . God's *arche* is the shared rule of equal persons in communion, not domination by some persons over other persons."[20]

The *koinonia* of the three persons of the Trinity extends beyond the inner life of God, to involve the people of God. Therefore the work of decision-making and administration of the church must be conducted collaboratively and collegially, centered in the *koinonia* of all the baptized people of God, both ordained and non-ordained. The bishops of the church, however, as leaders of the Christian community, oversee the processes of decision-making and administration by nurturing and safe-guarding the collegiality of the church which is grounded in the *koinonia* of the Christian community. The mandate for the leadership of the bishop is derived from the baptized people of God.[21] Each bishop is given the responsibility on

---

18. Volf, *After Our Likeness*, 217.

19. Volf, *After Our Likeness*, 217.

20. LaCugna, *God for Us*, 394.

21. This is a mandate in functional terms in which the people of God give assent to the leadership of the church. Ultimately the mandate for leadership in the church originates in God and is expressed in the person of Jesus through the power of the Holy Spirit. The instruction of Jesus to Peter, "Tend my sheep" (John 21:15–17) can be viewed in this light.

behalf of the baptized, for maintaining the alignment of the church to the faith that has been conveyed through the person and work of Jesus Christ, the apostles, and Christian disciples through the ages. Since the Christian community itself asks this responsibility of the bishop, and the bishop cannot hold this authority without the mandate of the baptized, that authority finally can be said to rest in the *koinonia* of the baptized people.

The baptized people of God must be involved in the decision-making procedures of the church through representatives who attend gatherings, councils, or synods in which decisions are made. It will be expedient in these processes of government that acknowledgement is paid to those who through their expertise, knowledge, experience, or pastoral gifts may be in a better position to make decisions than others.

A non-hierarchical structure of the ministry of the church sits in stark contrast with a hierarchical pyramidal conception of the church.

18

Ordained Ministry: A Focus of the Unity and Diversity of God

THE MINISTRY OF THE Roman Catholic Church ought to be diverse. The ordained ministry in particular ought to manifest both unity and diversity. The implications of this claim are that the ministry include people of many cultures and classes, women as well as men, and not just those vowed to a celibate lifestyle.

The doctrine of the Trinity affirms that the three persons, the Source of all that is, the eternal Word, and the Holy Spirit, are diverse, but also united in mutual love. The diversity and distinctiveness of the three persons is held in tension with the essential oneness of God. This quality of diversity within unity provides a foundation for viewing the ministry of the church, as diverse but essentially one.

There is only one ministry of the Christian church originating in the person and work of Jesus of Nazareth and ongoing through the power of the Spirit of God. Nevertheless this ministry is ideally as diverse as the gifts given to the baptized members of the church. Furthermore, the public ministry of the church is not and cannot be contained within the ordained ministry. Feminist theologian Ann Graff rightly argues for a diverse ministry. "If ministry is not simply going to shift to another core of elite persons, again separate from the community, we need to keep in mind the women's vision of a truly inclusive church of multiple kinds of ministry."[1]

---

1. Graff, "Women in the Roman Catholic Ministry," 227.

Ordained Ministry: A Focus of the Unity and Diversity of God

The interaction of many diverse ministries in the church gives form to the variety of gifts empowered by the Spirit. Paul's letter to the Corinthians indicated both the variety of gifts given for the building up of the community and the one source of those gifts:

> Now there are varieties of gifts, but the same Spirit; and there are varieties of services, but the same Lord; and there are varieties of activities, but it is the same God who activates all of them in everyone. To each is given the manifestation of the Spirit for the common good. To one is given through the Spirit the utterance of wisdom, and to another the utterance of knowledge according to the same Spirit, to another faith by the same Spirit, to another gifts of healing by the one Spirit, to another the working of miracles, to another prophecy, to another the discernment of spirits, to another various kinds of tongues, to another the interpretation of tongues. All these are activated by one and the same Spirit, who allots to each one individually just as the Spirit chooses. (1 Cor 12:4–11)

Miroslav Volf has good grounds for arguing that the church was founded through the presence of Christ in the Holy Spirit and "is constituted by way of the entire called and charismatically endowed people of God."[2] This is how Christ acts in our world today: through the gifts of the Spirit that are bestowed not only upon the ordained but upon all of the baptized: "This is why a division into those who serve in the congregation and those who are served is ecclesiologically unacceptable; every person is to serve with his or her specific gifts and every person is to be served in his or her specific need."[3]

I am not suggesting that all of the baptized are ministers, but rather that the gifts of ministry are so dispersed amongst the baptized that the work of ministry cannot be contained within the ordained ministry. A concrete example of ministerial gifts bestowed both in and beyond the ordained ministry is the ministry of prophecy that often arises where it is least expected. It cannot be contained in the ordained ministry. The ministry of the church must include the work of ordained and unordained ministers. The one ministry is fundamentally diverse and cannot be understood as contained within an all-male, celibate priesthood.

Furthermore, the *ordained* ministry itself ought to be understood as diverse within its unity and ought to reflect the diversity of the Christian

---

2. Volf, *After Our Likeness*, 228.
3. Volf, *After Our Likeness*, 230.

community from which it arises. Since its specific distinguishing role is the representation of the local church to the universal church and conversely the representation of the universal church to the local community, the ordained ministry must adequately reflect the diversity of the people whom it is representing. In this way the ordained ministry maintains and consolidates the unity and the diversity of the church. It must include people of many races, cultures, and classes, women as well as men, and both celibate and non-celibate peoples.

Anne Carr suggests a much more inclusive policy in the ordaining of ministers:

> Because it [ordained ministry] would include in its pastoral, liturgical, and social expressions a full representation of classes, races, and sexes, it would witness to its belief in "neither Greek nor Jew, slave nor free, male nor female." . . . The mutual involvement of men and women in the sacramental ministry would be an intrinsic sign of the service of unity required by the gospel.[4]

There is symbolic importance in the church ordaining both women and men. Such an act would affirm the full personhood of both women and men. Carr rightly argues that if we understand the church as a sacrament of Christ's incarnation amongst humankind, then it ought to express the mutuality of men and women and its service to all people by ordaining both women and men. This would enable "a fuller sacrament of the one priesthood of Christ in the whole People of God and of the apostolic witness of the message of Jesus to both men and women."[5]

Since it is already the case that women as well as men are involved in the pastoral ministry of the church, it is not appropriate that women be excluded in principle from the ordained ministry. As Carr again explains: "As long as women are barred from full recognition and sacramental completion of the service they are already fulfilling, barred in fact from the liturgical functions usually assigned to eight-year-old boys, the language of the church is unfortunately clear in what it is saying to women and to the world about women."[6]

Alternatively, if women were to be included amongst the ordained, the diversity of the ministry would be more fully acknowledged both sacramentally and practically.

4. Carr, *Transforming Grace*, 38–39.
5. Carr, *Transforming Grace*, 36.
6. Carr, *Transforming Grace*, 39.

In honoring its diversity, the ordained ministry must also include those who have not undertaken a celibate lifestyle. Those who come to the ministry of the church out of experiences of Christian marriage, human partnership, sexual engagement, childbearing, and child-rearing bring to that ministry depths of understanding human experience that cannot be present in a solely masculine and celibate ministry. That is not to say that all ministers need to have experienced the whole gamut of possibilities to be of pastoral worth, but the wholesale *exclusion* from the ministry of people other than celibate males is fundamentally diminishing.

The ordained ministry ought to reflect the diversity of culture that exists amongst the baptized people of God. This ought to involve an openness to the needs of various cultures and national groups and an openness to cultural variations in liturgical practice and customs. These various ways of expressing the one faith deserve to be celebrated, for they add to the richness of the universal church.

An opening of the ordained ministry to a greater diversity of ministers will result in expansion of the ordained ministry. Schillebeeckx went so far as to suggest a fourth order of ministry, in addition to the episcopate, presbyterate, and diaconate, in which pastoral workers were ordained. Pastoral workers ought to be incorporated into the ordained ministry, since many of them are already involved in work that has or ought to have a sacramental dimension. However, there is no reason why they could not be ordained into the present threefold ministry. To institute a fourth ministry seems an unnecessary action that has the potential to create division.

Ann Graff, too, argues for an expansion of the ordained ministry rather than a reduction. She rightly argues that "the cultic priesthood itself is a reduction of a broader embodiment of the ministry of Jesus, especially as *diakonia*."[7] An expansion of the ordained ministry would have the advantage of providing a larger and more diverse group of people who would serve local communities, also enabling ordained persons to engage in a greater variety of pastoral, political, or prophetic tasks. This would alleviate the narrowing of the tasks of the ordained into the cultic and liturgical functions. It may arise that in any one parish or community, there are two or three ordained persons who engage in a variety of ministerial tasks, one of which is presiding at the Eucharist. In summary, the ministry ought to be both diverse but one, manifesting the nature of God as three diverse persons united in the one God.

---

7. Graff, "Women in the Roman Catholic Ministry," 224.

19

Ordained Ministry: Manifesting the Ecstasy of God

IN THE VEIN OF LaCugna and Johnson, I suggest that the triune God does not remain apart from the whole of creation but is so related to all that is, that all of creation is caught up in the life of God. LaCugna explains: "God goes forth from God, God creates the world, God suffuses its history and dwells within us, redeeming the world from within."[1] She continues: "there is no rest (*stasis*) in *ek-stasis*, only continual movement outward."[2] The life of God shows forth mutual and just relationships and continually reaches outward to embrace all of creation, inviting the wider society to a loving, mutual, and just way of being. Wherever there are distorted relationships, whether between people, races, and sexes, or between the human community and the rest of creation, the life of the Trinity acts to challenge them. Where there are relationships of domination and subjection or of abuse, the life of the Trinity stands as a critique in its revelation of radical relationality and mutual love. It is by the power of grace, asserts Johnson, that "the trinitarian mystery of God actually empowers relationships of mutuality, equality and inclusiveness among persons and between human beings and the earth."[3]

---

1. LaCugna, *God for Us*, 353.
2. LaCugna, *God for Us*, 351.
3. LaCugna, *God for Us*, 351.

Ordained Ministry: Manifesting the Ecstasy of God

The ministry of the church, and the ordained ministry in particular, in manifesting the ecstatic life of God will similarly be caught up in the life of the community and will call the wider society to a loving, mutual, and just way of being. It will also be open to the call of the wider society for right relationship.

The work of Christian ministry, *if it is to embody the life of God*, will reach out beyond itself. It will both influence and be influenced by the wider human community of which it is a part. Christian ministry must hold in tension its own openness to the diversity of the human community and a vision for the fullness of humanity. The impact of Christian ministers upon the community might involve challenging but never dominating or coercing others towards a particular point of view. Christian ministry will influence and be influenced by others when it strives to establish equal and mutual relationships in which each party grows in its sense of identity and personhood. In manifesting the ecstatic nature of the triune God, ordained Christian ministers, who represent the church, neither lose their own unique sense of purpose nor subjugate others. The diversity and differences amongst the human community become a resource for human learning to be celebrated and protected. In this movement beyond itself, the Christian church is called to greater ecumenism. If the Roman Catholic Church, or indeed any other denominational church, is to be open to renewal and change, it will be important to acknowledge the work of the Spirit in other Christian denominations, recognizing not only Christian baptism in each church but also other forms of Christian ministry. The Christian churches are invited by the Spirit to give concrete form to the unity and communion that is at the heart of Christianity. As Schillebeeckx rightly argues, "the scandal is not that there are differences [between the Christian churches] but that these differences are used as an obstacle to communion."[4]

It is because the very life of God reveals mutual, loving, and just relationship that God can call forth the same from the people of God. How important it is then that the leadership of the church together with the baptized embody right relationships amongst themselves. If mutual and just relationships are not present in the life of the church, then the church lacks credibility in calling for right relationship in the wider society. It is the enactment or embodiment of God's way of being amongst the community that will have ecstatic affect. The manifestation of God's life by the

---

4. Schillebeeckx, *Church*, 197.

Part Three—Revisioning The Ordained Ministry

baptized cannot help but extend beyond itself, calling forth right relationship amongst all beings.

When the ministry of the church and the ordained ministry in particular is caught up in the life of the community and when it calls the wider society to a loving, mutual, and just way of being, it acts prophetically. The prophetic dimension of ministry is oriented towards the hope of the future and towards a vision of what might be. It is exemplified in Schillebeeckx's discussions of the "negative experiences of contrast"[5] in which people resist the suffering and oppression of our world because they know in the depths of their being that there is a possibility of a better world. Schillebeeckx argues that all people, Christians and agnostics alike, share this experience of "openness to the unknown and the better."[6]

---

5. Schillebeeckx, *Church*, 5.
6. Schillebeeckx, *Church*, 5–6.

20

The Need for the Democratization of the Church

SINCE THE TRIUNE GOD is three persons in mutual relationship and non-hierarchical in structure, there are good grounds for suggesting that the ministry of the church. and the ordained ministry in particular. ought to be structured non-hierarchically and in a way that promotes collegiality and collaboration amongst the baptized people of God. However, a more collaborative form of ministry as I have described can only emerge if the Roman Catholic Church embraces democratization.

It is important to acknowledge that there are many understandings of the notion of democracy and democratization. In speaking of the need for the democratization of the church, I am suggesting changes in church structure and government that would allow for the participation of all the baptized, by representation, in the decision-making procedures of the church.

Edward Schillebeeckx has rightly critiqued the notion of a divinely-willed hierarchical structure which precludes democratic structures within the church,[1] and he advocates a more democratic form of church government in *Church: The Human Story of God*. He argues that there are intrinsic

---

1. Schillebeeckx's critique of hierarchy is evident throughout *The Church with a Human Face*, and this critique is furthered in the later *Church: the Human Story of God*. In the latter text, he critiques the notion of a divinely willed hierarchy which does not allow democratic procedure, describing it as "an historical misunderstanding." He argues for "the participation of all believers in decisions relating to church government" (188–213).

ecclesiological reasons for "preferring a democratic exercise of ministerial authority in the church to oligarchical, monarchical or feudal forms of government."[2] He argues firstly that the Holy Spirit is at work in the church, "generally and specifically in all the people of God and in a specific ministerial way in the official activity of the church leaders."[3] The Christian community as a whole needs to be open to the various channels of the Spirit, and this is best achieved through the democratic participation of all the baptized in the decision-making processes of the church. Secondly, Schillebeeckx reminds his readers that God's rule, revealed through the life, ministry, death, and resurrection of Jesus Christ, is "non-authoritarian, vulnerable and even helpless."[4] God has been revealed in history as one who is not authoritarian but rather values and respects human freedom. The democratization of the church therefore ought not to be feared but rather viewed as a way of openness to God's ways. Finally, Schillebeeckx argues that the Spirit of God works in a myriad of ways in the church and for this reason, the Christian church needs to be open to the interdependence of theology, of ministry, and of the believing community itself.[5]

Many other theologians also call for more democratic processes of decision-making in the church and for changes in church structure that would ensure that all baptized people participate in the decision-making procedures of the church. Eugene Bianchi and Rosemary Radford Ruether, like Schillebeeckx, challenge the assumption that the church has always possessed a centralized and monarchical government given to it by Jesus Christ.[6] Through the work of historical retrieval, scholars have demonstrated that the earliest Christian communities had a strong egalitarian stance in which the gifts of all the baptized people of God were valued and in which women as well as men were involved in the ministry and leadership of the church. "[D]emocratic elements have always existed in the past in certain aspects of church government, and . . . democratic polity suits the theological meaning of the church as redemptive society better than does monarchical hierarchy."[7]

---

2. Schillebeeckx, *Church*, 220.
3. Schillebeeckx, *Church*, 220
4. Schillebeeckx, *Church*, 221.
5. Schillebeeckx, *Church*, 228.
6. Bianchi and Ruether, *Democratic Catholic Church*, 7.
7. Bianchi and Ruether, *Democratic Catholic Church*, 7.

The Need for the Democratization of the Church

Bianchi and Ruether introduce a theological argument for the democratization of the church, one that Schillebeeckx hints at in his suggestion that the church is "called to life" through the non-powerful rule of God.[8] They suggest, "The church should witness to what is most redemptive in human relations: just, loving and truthful relationality that fosters mutual respect. A church that has become a paradigm of the opposite of all these traits falls below, rather than rises above, the "world" to which it is sent to speak God's saving word."[9]

It is important to address the often made comment that the church cannot be a democracy and should not be viewed in the same light as the governing of a democratic nation.[10] Many critics of the call for the democratization of the church, who rightly point out that the church is founded through the inspiration of the Spirit of God, go on to incorrectly conclude that for this reason, decision-making is best left in the hands of the church hierarchy. The fact that the church is divinely willed, does not preclude democratic process. The issue under debate is not that the church is founded by the Spirit and that the will of God ought to be heeded, but rather *how* the church discerns the will of God or the work of the Spirit. The processes of discerning God's will for the church ought to be based in the *koinonia* of the believing community.

A second common objection is that because the church has a threefold structure of order it cannot be a democracy. I have shown that a threefold order of ministry can be understood in a non-hierarchical and relational way. Decision-making ought not be restricted to an elite group in the church but rather be opened to a wider body that represents the whole of the people of God, the universal church, and its diverse peoples.

---

8. Schillebeeckx, *Church*, 222.

9. Bianchi and Ruether, *Democratic Catholic Church*, 11.

10. John Coleman, for example, argues in "Not Democracy but Democratization" that "The church is not, in any formal sense, a democracy since ultimate sovereignty does not rest with the people" and rightly attributes the institution of the church to the will of Christ (Bianchi and Ruether, *Democratic Catholic Church*, 226). However I would argue that so too in any nation, democratic or otherwise, ultimate sovereignty does not rest with the people either. The realm of God is not confined to the church. There is a danger here in using one set of principles to speak about governing a nation and another about governing the church. Schillebeeckx has discussed this dilemma and pointed out how readily Pius XII condemned state absolutism but carefully distinguished this from the "absolute monarchy" of the church (*Church*, 204). I suggest that ultimate sovereignty in the church ought not to rest in the people but in God. Nevertheless, the will of God can only begin to be discerned by heeding the concerns of all, especially the silent.

Part Three—Revisioning The Ordained Ministry

The non-hierarchical, equal, and mutual mode of relating which is revealed in the three persons of the Trinity ought to be given expression in the ministry of the church. The doctrine of the Trinity provides theological underpinning for advocating the democratization of the church. The qualities of the triune God, whilst not suggesting any specific forms of church organization, suggest a general principle of democratic process which might guide the church in its future organization.

The notion that all of the baptized be involved in the life, mission, and ministry of the church and be co-responsible for the work of building up the Christian community is consonant with the equal and mutual mode of relating revealed in the triune God. As confirmed in the previous chapter, all ministry is grounded in baptism. All Christians have a responsibility arising out of the promises made in baptism to work as Christian disciples towards the building up of the Christian church. This does not mean that all of the baptized need to carry out ministerial works themselves, but to ensure that the ministry of the church is undertaken by those who are called and gifted to do so.

The democratization of the church would see the inclusion by representation of non-ordained members of the church in the decision-making procedures. Representatives from various communities, dioceses, and countries would meet together in council or synod. The view that work of this nature rightly belongs only to ordained ministers is one that feminist scholars, Schillebeeckx and others, critique. Karl Rahner, for example, argues, "A more obvious participation of the laity is required, not only in the appointment of office-holders, but also in other decision-making processes in the life of the Church."[11] The notion that the laity ought to be primarily responsible for temporal affairs and the ordained ministry responsible for the affairs of the church needs to be challenged. The laity must be involved in the affairs of the church and ordained ministers must take up their role as responsible citizens in the wider community.

Church government needs to be open to the voice of the prophets wherever they speak. Since prophecy can arise in many unlikely places, this will necessitate an openness to voices outside of the formal ministry of the church and even outside of the Christian community itself. The ministers of the church, as much as is humanly possible, must manifest something of the ecstatic nature of God by looking outwards beyond themselves, both affecting and being affected by the wider society. Similarly, church

---

11. Rahner, *Shape of the Church*, 121.

The Need for the Democratization of the Church

government ought to ponder the calls in the wider society for democratic political process. In previous periods, such at the close of World War II, the church has condemned state absolutism and called for more democratic political processes within nations, processes which the church is not prepared to embrace itself.[12] This is a particularly sensitive issue today, when there is, with just cause, a great suspicion of monarchical absolutism around the globe.[13] Church government, whilst it cannot and ought not cave in to every demand or political movement, must be attentive to the signs of the times, which in this instance, includes the worldwide call for more democratic and participatory national governments. This reality ought to be food for thought in a church that continues to insist upon monarchical rule.

Those involved in the ministry and decision-making procedures of the church must be accountable to the whole of the believing community, but likewise the believing community must take up their baptismal responsibility in facilitating and ensuring that the ministry and decision-making processes of the church are carried on. To be co-responsible for the mission and ministry of the church means that both ordained and non-ordained ministers work together in an environment of equality and mutuality. As Graff argues, "a collaborative church does not simply name a style of advisory conversation to benefit church governors, but is a way of being church together."[14]

Schillebeeckx is right to suggest that although Vatican II went some way toward making the participation of the baptized possible in encouraging the formation of national, diocesan, and pastoral councils, the work of these bodies, has been "undermined from above and tamed."[15] If there are to be democratic practices operating in the church, they need to be safeguarded institutionally.

Hans Küng, although advocating a strong role of leadership for ordained ministers, also saw a need for co-responsibility for ministry. He argued that both the community and community-leaders ought to share responsibility for the life of the church: "The leader whose vocation has

---

12. On Christmas Eve, 1944, Pius XII issued an address, *Nuntius radiophonicus: ai populi del mondo intero*, in which he criticized state absolutism, although distinguishing it from absolute monarchy, which functions in the church (*AAS* 37 (10–23): 11–17).

13. Schillebeeckx, *Church*, 188.

14. Graff, "Women in the Roman Catholic Ministry," 218.

15. Schillebeeckx, *Church*, 209.

been publicly examined, leads in the Spirit of the Christian message the community, which always shares the responsibility with the leader."[16]

John Coleman notes that Patrick Granfield has argued for a church that is accountable to its people:

> On a practical level, the bureaucratic system of the church diminishes its legitimation when it neglects consultation, collaboration, accountability and due process and when it assumes an adversarial and negative attitude. An overly monarchical and centralized bureaucracy distances itself from the faithful and loses its contact with urgent pastoral needs. Administrative procedures and management styles have to be critically assessed, in order to avoid the undesirable aspects of bureaucracy such as inflexibility, cumbersomeness, inefficiency and unfairness.[17]

A specific function that requires restoration through the democratization of the church is the role of the community in the choice of its ministers, a work in which all of the baptized members of the church need to be involved. Schillebeeckx has argued this, drawing from the data of history and demonstrating that the early church was involved in this process. By grounding his ecclesiology in a trinitarian foundation, Miroslav Volf arrives at a similar conclusion; that is, that the whole congregation must participate in the election of office-holders:

> That office-holders can and should be elected is grounded in the character of the charismata of office, that is, in their essential attachment to a concrete local church. That the members of a local church can and should elect office-holders is grounded in their calling and in their baptism. All those who are baptized share responsibility for the church and thus must be able to participate in church decisions, including the election of office-holders.[18]

Margaret Ulloa, in a similar vein as Schillebeeckx, argues decisively for a return to the earlier practice of the church in which communities proposed to the bishop for ordination, people who emerged in the community as natural leaders or people "who are perceived by the community as having the requisite gifts or who feel called to offer this service to their own brothers and sisters."[19]

16. Küng, *Why Priests?*, 27.
17. Granfield cited in Bianchi and Ruether, *Democratic Catholic Church*, 229.
18. Volf, *After Our Likeness*, 255.
19. Ulloa, "Extending Ordained Ministry," 11.

The Need for the Democratization of the Church

Rosemary Ruether too, argued that the processes of both selecting and educating the ordained ministry should arise "from within the self-educative process of the community itself."[20] She envisaged the community first reflecting on its particular mission and then in response designating "especially talented and committed persons"[21] for teaching, pastoral, and leadership roles within the community. Ruether understands that it is essentially the community itself that ordains a person. Whilst the community must be involved in the ordination of their leader, so too must the wider church, since the role of the ordained person will be to represent the church. It is both the community and the wider church who must collaborate to ordain its ministers.

In 1972, Karl Rahner, in his reflections upon the church of the future, could foresee that the future church would be "one built from below by basic communities as a result of free initiative and association," and as such these communities "have just as much right as a territorial parish to be recognized as a basic element of the church."[22] Furthermore, Rahner argued, "When such a community exists, coming from below, formed through the free decision of faith of its members, it has the right to be recognized as Church by the episcopal great Church and to have its community leader recognized by the great Church through ordination."[23] This ordination would be a relative rather than an absolute ordination, assigning the ordained person only to their particular community. Written more than forty years ago, Rahner's reflections also imagined that this ordained leader of the community may be married. He proposed that the question might also be asked whether a woman could be considered for leadership of a basic community and therefore be ordained to the priestly office and concludes, "I see no reason in principle to give a negative answer to this question."[24]

I have argued for the democratization of the Roman Catholic Church, a process that would protect the role of the community in choosing its ministers and enable the whole of the baptized community to engage in the decision-making processes of the church. The democratization of the church is theologically underpinned by the notion that the church ought to

---

20. Ruether cited in Harris, "Questioning Lay Ministry," 108.
21. Ruether, cited inHarris, "Questioning Lay Ministry," 108.
22. Rahner, *Shape of the Church*, 108–9.
23. Rahner, *Shape of the Church*, 108–9.
24. Rahner, *Shape of the Church*, 114.

Part Three—Revisioning The Ordained Ministry

embody the equal and mutual mode of relating that is revealed in the life of the triune God.

I have offered here a vision of ordained ministry that is grounded in the context of the mission and ministry of the universal church. The ordained ministry must embody as much as is humanly possible, the life of the triune God. It must be a ministry based in mutual and just relationship between all persons and though there is only one ministry, it must embody the diversity of the Christian community. The ordained ministry must therefore work to maintain and consolidate both the unity and the diversity of the Christian church. Finally, it must be non-hierarchical and embody the ecstatic nature of God: that is, it must move beyond itself for the fullness of relationship.

21

Conclusion

I BEGAN IN CHAPTER 1 by referring to the present crisis in the ministry of the Roman Catholic Church and within the ordained ministry itself. It is a crisis about which many have written from a variety of perspectives. Throughout this book I have argued from a feminist standpoint, engaging methodologies consonant with feminist practice and using the writings of a number of key feminist theologians.

A springboard for constructing a new approach to the theology of ministry is the work of Edward Schillebeeckx, chiefly his revised work on ministry, and *The Church with a Human Face*. Schillebeeckx's writing, as I have shown, makes a considerable contribution in critiquing the current practices and theology of ordained ministry in the Roman Catholic Church. His approach is to survey the history of the tradition, pointing out that change has been an intrinsic and even necessary aspect of the tradition, and one which can be of benefit to the church. However, Schillebeeckx's work can be taken further: I have used the contributions of feminist liberation theologies to pursue some of the issues that Schillebeeckx raises and to ask further questions about the practice and theology of the ordained ministry.

In order to arrive at a revisioned theology of ordained ministry, I have critiqued the tradition and theology of the ministry and retrieved from the tradition those practices, memories, and stories that can be used as a resource for revisioning. I have achieved this by exploring the writings of Schillebeeckx through the lens of feminist theology.

Part Three—Revisioning The Ordained Ministry

I have stated that many of the practices and perspectives of the tradition actually hinder rather than assist the church's work of ministry. The official ministry of the Roman Catholic Church has not been helped by a theology that has set it apart from and elevated it above the Christian community. I have challenged the notion that the ordained minister alone has sacred power to act in the community: rather sacred power is apprehended by the gathered community, albeit through the liturgical leadership of an ordained minister.

The hierarchical structure of the ordained ministry has over the years served to disempower the wider baptized community of the Roman Catholic Church. I have suggested that the traditional notion that the ordained minister is bestowed with a special ontological character needs reinterpretation in terms of the relationship between the minister and the Christian community. Furthermore, I have proposed that the commitment to the ordained ministry need not be lifelong.

I have challenged the church's teaching about priestly representation, arguing that the distinctive and primary role of the ordained person is to represent the church, that is, to stand *in persona ecclesia*. The ordained ministry ought to act to consolidate and maintain both the unity and diversity of the church. Along with all of the baptized faithful, ministers also stand *in persona Christi*. Catholic people must challenge the lack of involvement of the community in selecting ministers. They must challenge the requirement of celibacy for the ordained ministry and importantly, they must challenge the exclusion of women from the ordained ministry of the church.

I have retrieved practices, memories, and stories from the tradition to show that the history of Christianity is indeed a history of women as well as men. I have aimed to restore to history the story of the egalitarian nature of the early church and the story of women's leadership in the early church. I have shown the importance of retrieving the prophetic voice of women and I make a plea for retrieving the significance of Christian baptism. I have argued for a reinterpretation of the notion of *diakonia*, since the notion of servanthood is problematic for many women and disenfranchised persons in the church. In summary, I have argued that a reinterpretation of the doctrine of the Trinity will provide a theological underpinning for freshly understanding Christian ministry and the ordained ministry itself.

In this book, I have put forward a reconstructed theology of the ordained ministry that is grounded in trinitarian theology. If trinitarian faith is to be lived, as Catherine LaCugna has rightly argued, then the symbol of the Trinity ought to be not merely imitated but actually embodied in the ministry and the ordained ministry of the church. The ordained ministry must embody God's collaborative, mutual, and non-hierarchical way of being, thus sharing the responsibility for ministry with the non-ordained of the church.

The ordained ministry must also, as much as is humanly possible, embody the relationality of the triune God, valuing and nurturing mutual and interdependent relationships amongst the baptized.

I have argued that the ordained ministry must embody both the unity and diversity of the triune God. Though unified in their proclamation of the realm of God, revealed in the person of Jesus Christ, Christian ministers ought to manifest the diversity that is present in the human community. Ministers might manifest diversity that is present in race, culture, class, sex, and age as well as in the gifts and skills they bring to ministry.

Just as the triune God does not remain apart from creation, the ordained ministry itself needs to embody this ecstatic desire, by its movement outward toward not only the wider Christian community but to a care for all persons and creation itself. It will invite the wider society to a more loving, mutual, and just way of being and be open to the concerns and critique that the wider society brings to it.

If the Christian ministry and the ordained ministry in particular is to live a trinitarian faith by embodying the very life of God, then it is clearly necessary that it become more democratic. Structures need to be in place which enable and indeed protect the capacity of the baptized people of God to be fully involved in the decision-making processes of the church.

This reconstructed theology of the ordained ministry is not an end in itself. As LaCugna rightly concluded, "the nature of the church should manifest the nature of God."[1] The task of the ordained ministry is to consciously and as much as is humanly possible embody the life of God to the end that the life of the people of God, indeed the life of all God's creation is enhanced, honored, and brought to its fullness.

---

1. LaCugna, *God for Us*, 403.

Bibliography

Abbott, Walter M., ed. *The Documents of Vatican II*. London: Geoffrey Chapman, 1966.
Armstrong, Karen. *The End of Silence: Women and Priesthood*. London: Fourth Estate, 1993.
Becker, Carol E. "Women in Church Leadership—In but still Out." *Dialog* 35 (1966) 144–48.
Béguerie, Philippe. *How to Understand the Sacraments*. London: SCM, 1991.
Bernier, Paul. *Ministry in the Church: A Historical and Pastoral Approach*. Mystic, CT: Twenty-Third, 1996.
Bianchi, Eugene C., and Rosemary Radford Ruether. *A Democratic Catholic Church: The Reconstruction of Roman Catholicism*. New York: Crossroad, 1993.
Bloomquist, Karen. "The Ordained Woman: Embarrassment or Gift?" In *Women and Religion: a Reader for the Clergy*, edited by Regina Coll, 71–80. New York: Paulist, 1982.
Boff, Leonardo. "Matters Requiring Clarification: Is the Distinction between *ecclesia docens* and *ecclesia discens* Justified?" In *Who has the Say in the Church?* edited by Marcus Lefébure, 47. New York: Seabury, 1981.
Bowden, John. *Edward Schillebeeckx: Portrait of a Theologian*. London: SCM, 1983.
Bowie, Fiona, and Oliver Davies, eds. *Hildegard of Bingen: An Anthology*. London: SPCK, 1990.
Brown, Neil, ed. *Faith and Culture: Challenges in Ministry*. Sydney: Catholic Institute of Sydney, 1989.
Brown, Raymond E., and John P. Meier. *Antioch and Rome: New Testament Cradles of Catholic Christianity*. London: Geoffrey Chapman, 1983.
Bührig, Marga. "The Role of Women in the Ecumenical Dialogue." In *Women-Invisible in Theology and Church*, edited by Elisabeth Schüssler Fiorenza et al., 91–100. Edinburgh: T. & T. Clark, 1985
Butler, Sara. "Forum: Ordaining Women." *Worship* 63.1 (1989) 467–71.
———. "Forum: Second Thoughts on Ordaining Women." *Worship* 63.2 (1989) 157–65.
———. "Quaestio Disputata: in Persona Christi: A Response to Dennis Ferrara." *Theological Studies* 56 (1995) 61–80.
———. "Women's Ordination and the Development of Doctrine." *The Thomist* 61 (1997) 501–24.
Byrnes, Jenny. "Women Clergy in Leadership—A Review of Literature." *Australian Ministry* (1990) 14–16.

Bibliography

Carr, Anne. *Transforming Grace: Christian Experience and Women's Experience.* San Francisco: Harper & Row, 1988.
Carr, Anne, and Elisabeth Schüssler Fiorenza, eds. *The Special Nature of Women?* London: SCM, 1991.
———. "The New Vision of Feminist Theology". In *Freeing Theology: The Essentials of Theology in Feminist Perspective*, edited by Catherine Mowry LaCugna, 5–29. San Francisco: HarperSanFrancisco, 1993.
Carroll, Sandra. "Remembering her: An Exploration of the Method of Elisabeth Schüssler Fiorenza." *Compass* 29.1 (1995) 10–14.
Catechism of the Catholic Church. Libreria Editrice Vaticana. Homebush, NSW: St. Paul, 1995.
Catherine of Siena. *The Dialogue.* Translated by Suzanne Noffke. London: SPCK, 1980.
Chantraine, Georges. "Apostolicity according to Schillebeeckx: The Notion and its Import." *Communio* 12 (1985) 192–222.
Chirico, Peter. Review: *The Church with a Human Face*, by Edward Schillebeeckx. *Theological Studies* 47 (1986) 158–59.
Chopp, Rebecca. "In the Real World: A Feminist Theology for the Church." *Quarterly Review* 16 (1996) 3–22.
———. *The Power to Speak: Feminism, Language and God.* New York: Crossroad, 1991.
Coleman, John A. *The Evolution of Dutch Catholicism, 1958-74.* Berkeley and Los Angeles: University of California Press, 1978.
———. "Not Democracy but Democratization." In *A Democratic Catholic Church: The Reconstruction of Roman Catholicism*, edited by Eugene C. Bianchi and Rosemary Radford Ruether, 80–93. New York: Crossroad, 1992.
Coll, Regina, ed. *Women and Religion: A Reader for the Clergy.* New York: Paulist, 1982.
Collins, John N. *Are All Christians Ministers?* Sydney: E. J. Dwyer, 1992.
Collins, Mary. "Is the eucharist still a source of meaning for women?" *Origins* 21 (1991) 225–29.
———. "Principles of Feminist Liturgy." In *Women at Worship: Interpretations of North American Diversity*, edited by Marjorie Proctor Smith and Janet R. Walton, 9–26. Louisville, KY: Westminster/John Knox, 1993.
———. "The Refusal of Women in Clerical Circles." In *Women in the Church*, edited by Madonna Kolbenschlag, 51–63. Washington, DC: Pastoral, 1987.
———. *Worship: Renewal to Practice.* Washington, DC: Pastoral, 1987.
Condren, Mary. *The Serpent and the Goddess: Women, Religion and Power in Celtic Ireland.* New York: Harper Collins, 1989.
Congar, Yves. *Lay People in the Church.* London: Geoffrey Chapman, 1957.
Congregation for the Clergy. *Directory on the Ministry and Life of Priests.* Rome: Libreria Editrice Vaticana, 1994.
Cooper, Austin. *Julian of Norwich: Reflections on Selected Texts.* Homebush, NSW: St. Paul, 1986.
Cullinan, Edmond. "Forum: women and the diaconate." *Worship* 70 (1996) 260–66.
Daly, Mary. *The Church and the Second Sex.* New York: Harper & Row, 1975.
———. "Theology after the Demise of God the Father: A Call for the Castration of Sexist Religion." In *Sexist Religion and Women in the Church: No More Silence!*, edited by Alice L. Hageman, 125–42. New York: Association, 1974.
Denzinger, Henricus. *Enchiridion Symbolorum: Definitionum et Declarationum de Rebus Fidei et Morum.* Rome: Herder, 1965.

Dewey, Joanna. "The Gospel of Mark." In *Searching the Scriptures, Vol. 2.*, edited by Elisabeth Schüssler Fiorenza, 470–509. New York: Crossroad, 1994.

Donovan, Daniel. Review of *Church: The Human Story of God, The Church with a Human Face*, by Edward Schillebeeckx. *New Theology Review* 7 (1994) 90–91.

———. *What are they Saying about the Ministerial Priesthood?* New York: Paulist, 1992.

Douglass, Jane Dempsey. "Women and the Continental Reformation." In *Religion and Sexism: Images of Women in the Jewish and Christian Traditions*, edited by Rosemary Radford Ruether, 292–318. New York: Simon and Schuster, 1974.

Douglas, Mary. "A modest proposal: a place for women in the hierarchy." *Commonweal* (1996) 12–15.

Downey, Michael, ed. *That They Might Live: Power, Empowerment, and Leadership in the Church*. New York: Crossroad, 1991.

Downey, Michael, and Richard Fragomeni, eds. *A Promise of Presence: Studies in Honor of David N. Power OMI*. Washington, DC: Pastoral, 1992.

Dulles, Avery. *Models of the Church*. Dublin: Gill and MacMillan, 1976.

Durka, Gloria. "Is Partnership Possible? Ordained Men and Unordained Women in Ministry." In *Women and Religion: A Reader for the Clergy*, edited by Regina Coll, 45–59. New York: Paulist, 1982.

———. *Praying with Hildegard of Bingen*. Winona, MN: Saint Mary's, 1991.

Edwards, Denis. *Called to be Church in Australia: An Approach to the Renewal of Local Churches*. Homebush, NSW: St. Paul, 1987.

———. "Personal Symbol of Communion." In *The Spirituality of the Diocesan Priest*, edited by Donald B. Cozzens, 73–84. Collegeville, MN: Liturgical, 1997.

Eigo, Francis, ed. *A Discipleship of Equals: Towards a Christian Feminist Spirituality*. Pennsylvania: Villanova University Press, 1988.

Fackre, Gabriel. "Bones Strong and Weak in the Skeletal Structure of Schillebeeckx's Christology." *Journal of Ecumenical Studies* 21 (1984) 248–77.

Fairbanks, Sarah Ann. "Liturgical Preaching by Women: A New Sign Language of Salvation." *The Way Supplement* 83 (1995) 131–40.

Ferrara, Dennis Michael. "A reply to Sara Butler." *Theological Studies* 56 (1995) 81–91.

———. "Representation or Self-effacement? The Axiom *in persona Christi* in St Thomas and the Magisterium." *Theological Studies* 55 (1994) 195–224.

Field-Bibb, Jacqueline. *Women towards Priesthood: Ministerial Politics and Feminist Praxis*. Cambridge, UK: Cambridge University Press, 1991.

Fiorenza, Elisabeth Schüssler, ed. *But She Said: Feminist Practices of Biblical Interpretation*. Boston: Beacon, 1992.

———. *Discipleship of Equals*. London: SCM, 1993.

———. *In Memory of Her: A Feminist Theological Reconstruction of Christian Origins*. London: SCM, 1986.

———. *Jesus: Miriam's Child, Sophia's Prophet*. London: SCM, 1995.

———. *Searching the Scriptures, Vol. 2*. New York: Crossroad, 1994.

———. "Struggle is a Name for Hope: A Critical Feminist Interpretation for Liberation." *Colloquia on Feminist Hermeneutics* (1995).

———. "Tablesharing and the Celebration of the Eucharist." *Concilium* 152 (1982) 3–11.

———. "Waiting at Table: A Critical Feminist Theological Reflection on Diakonia." *Concilium* 198 (1988) 84–94.

———. *Women: Invisible in Church and Theology*. Edinburgh: T & T Clark, 1985.

Fiorenza, Francis Schüssler. *Foundational Theology: Jesus and the Church*. New York: Crossroad, 1984.

Bibliography

Fiorenza, Francis Schüssler, and John Galvin, eds. *Systematic Theology: Roman Catholic Perspectives, Vol. 1*. Minneapolis: Fortress, 1991.

Flick, Alexander. *The Decline of the Medieval Church, Vol. 2*. New York: Burt Franklin, 1967.

Ford, J. Massyngberde, "Women Leaders in the New Testament." In *Women Priests: A Catholic Commentary on the Vatican Declaration*, edited by Leonard Swidler, Leonard and Arlene Swidler, 132–34. New York: Paulist, 1977.

Fox, Patricia. "The Trinity as Transforming Symbol: Exploring the Trinitarian Theology of two Roman Catholic Feminist Theologians." *Pacifica* 7 (1994) 273–94.

Frohlich, Mary. "Schillebeeckx on Prayer: Politics, Mysticism and Liturgy." *Liturgy* 5 (1986) 35–39.

Gleeson, Gerald P., ed. *Priesthood: The Hard Questions*. Newtown, NSW: E. J. Dwyer, 1993.

Goosen, Gideon. "Ministries and the Theory of Goals." *Colloquium* (1996) 106–21.

Gössman, Elisabeth. "Women's Ordination and the Vatican." *Feminist Theology* 18 (1998) 67–86.

Graff, Ann O'Hara, ed. *In the Embrace of God: Feminist Approaches to Theological Anthropology*. New York: Orbis, 1995.

———. "Infallibility: Have We Heard the Final Word on Women's Ordination?" *US Catholic* 61 (1996) 6–13.

———. "Women in the Roman Catholic Ministry: New Vision, New Ethics." In *Clergy Ethics in a Changing Society: Mapping the Terrain*, edited by James P. Wind et al., 215–30. Louisville: Westminster/John Knox, 1991.

Grant, Jacquelyn. "Poverty, Womanist Theology and the Ministry of the Church." In *Standing with the Poor: Theological Reflections on Economic Reality*, edited by Paul Plenge Parker. Cleveland, OH: Pilgrim, 1991.

Grant, Robert, and David Tracy. *A Short History of the Interpretation of the Bible*. London: SCM, 1984.

Gray, Janette. *Neither Escaping nor Exploiting Sex*. Homebush. NSW: St Paul, 1995.

Grelot, Pierre. *Eglises et ministères: pour un dialogue critique avec Edward Schillebeeckx*. Paris: Cerf, 1983.

Grollenberg, Lucas, et al., *Minister? Pastor? Prophet? Grass Roots Leadership in the Churches*. London: SCM, 1980.

Groome, Thomas H. "From Chauvinism and Clericalism to Priesthood: The Long March." In *Women and Religion: A Reader for the Clergy*, edited by Regina Coll, 111–26. New York: Paulist, 1982.

Gudorf, Christine. "The Power to Create: Sacraments and Men's Need to Birth". *Horizons* 14.2 (1987) 296–309.

Gutierrez, Gustavo. *We Drink from Our Own Wells*. New York: Orbis, 1984

Hageman, Alice L., ed. *Sexist Religion and Women in the Church*. New York: Association, 1974.

Haight, Roger. *Dynamics of Theology*. New York: Paulist, 1990.

Hampson, Daphne. *Theology and Feminism*. Oxford: Blackwells, 1990.

Harrington, Wilfred. Review of *The Church with a Human Face*, by Edward Schillebeeckx. *Doctrine and Life* 36 (1986) 384.

Harris, Maria. "A Discipleship of Equals: Implications for Ministry." In *A Discipleship of Equals: Towards a Christian Feminist Spirituality*, edited by Francis A. Eigo, 151–72. Pennsylvania: Villanova University Press, 1988.

———. "Questioning Lay Ministry." In *Women and Religion: A Reader for the Clergy*, edited by Regina Coll, 97–110. New York: Paulist, 1982.

Heyer, Robert, ed. *Women and Orders.* New York: Paulist, 1974.
Hess, Carol Lakey. "Education as an Art of Getting Dirty with Dignity." In *The Arts of Ministry: Feminist-Womanist Approaches,* edited by Christie Cozad Neuger, 60–87. Louisville: Westminster/John Knox, 1996.
Hilkert, Mary Catherine. "Hermeneutics of History in the Theology of Edward Schillebeeckx." *The Thomist* 51 (1987) 97–145.
———. *Naming Grace: Preaching and the Sacramental Imagination.* New York: Continuum, 1997.
———. Review of *Church: The Human Story of God,* by Edward Schillebeeckx. *Horizons* 19 (1992) 325–26.
———. "The Word beneath the Words." In *A Promise of Presence: Studies in Honor of David Power,* edited by Michael Downey and Richard Fragomeni, 49–70. Washington, DC: Pastoral, 1992.
Hilkert, Mary Catherine and Robert Schreiter, eds. *The Praxis of Christian Experience: An Introduction to the Theology of Edward Schillebeeckx.* San Francisco: Harper & Row, 1989.
Hines, Mary E. "Community for Liberation: Church." In *Freeing Theology: The Essentials of Theology in Feminist Perspective,* edited by Catherine Mowry LaCugna, 161–84. San Francisco: HarperSanFrancisco, 1993.
———. "The Praxis of the Kingdom of God: Ministry." In *The Praxis of Christian Experience: An Introduction to the Theology of Edward Schillebeeckx,* edited by Robert J. Schreiter and Mary Catherine Hilkert, 116–30. San Francisco: Harper & Row, 1989.
Hunt, Mary. "Change or be Changed: Roman Catholicism and Violence." *Feminist Theology* 12 (1996) 43–60.
Husserl, Edmund. *Phenomenology and the Crisis of Philosophy.* New York: Harper & Row, 1965.
Hypher, Paul. "Future Models of Ordained Ministry." *The Way Supplement* 83 (1995) 91–108.
Isaacs, Marie E. "Priesthood and the Epistle to the Hebrews." *The Heythrop Journal* 38 (1997) 51–62.
Jeanrod, Werner G. Review of *The Church with a Human Face,* by Edward Schillebeeckx. *The Furrow* 37 (1986) 536–39.
John Paul II. *Apostolic Letter of his Holiness Pope John Paul II on Reserving Priestly Ordination to Men Alone.* Vatican City: Libreria Editrice, 1994.
———. *Instruction on Certain Questions Regarding the Collaboration of the Non-ordained Faithful in the Sacred Ministry of Priest.* Vatican City: Libreria Editrice, 1997.
Johnson, Elizabeth A. *Consider Jesus: Waves of Renewal in Christology.* London: Geoffrey Chapman, 1990.
———. *Friends of God and Prophets: A Feminist Theological Reading of the Communion of Saints.* London: SCM, 1998.
———. *She Who Is: The Mystery of God in Feminist Theological Discourse.* New York: Crossroad, 1994.
———. "Trinity: to let the Symbol Sing Again." *Theology Today* 54 (1997) 299–311.
Johnson, Elizabeth A., et al., "Current Theology: Feminist Theology: A Review of the Literature." *Theological Studies* 56 (1995) 327–52.
Kasper, Walter. "Ministry in the Church: Taking issue with Edward Schillebeeckx." *Communio* 10 (1983) 185–95.

Bibliography

Keifer, Ralph A. "Schillebeeckx on Ministry: Herald of a New Reformation." *Commonweal* 108 (1981) 401–3.

Kennedy, Philip. "Continuity underlying Discontinuity: Schillebeeckx's Philosophical Background." *New Blackfriars* 70 (1989) 264–77.

———. *Schillebeeckx*. London: Geoffrey Chapman, 1993.

Kerr, Fergus. Review of *Church: The Human Story of God*, by Edward Schillebeeckx. *New Blackfriars* 73 (1992) 571–73.

Kilmartin, Edward. "Apostolic Office: Sacrament of Christ." *Theological Studies* 36 (1975) 243–64.

———. "Office and Charism: Reflections on a New Study of Ministry." *Theological Studies* 38 (1977) 547–54.

———. "Sacraments as Liturgy of the Church." *Theological Studies* 50 (1989) 527–47.

Kolbenschlag, Madonna, ed. *Women in the Church*. Washington, DC: Pastoral, 1987.

Komonchak, Joseph, et al., eds. *New Dictionary of Theology*. Dublin: Gill and McMillan, 1987.

Küng, Hans. "Participation of the Laity in Church Leadership and in Church Elections." In *A Democratic Catholic Church: The Reconstruction of Roman Catholicism*, edited by Eugene C. Bianchi and Rosemary Radford Ruether, 80–93. New York: Crossroad, 1992.

———. *Theology for the Third Millenium: An Ecumenical View*. New York: Doubleday, 1988.

———. *Why Priests?* London: William Collins, 1972.

———. "Women's Ordination/Infallibility: Theologians now face either-or Situation." *National Catholic Reporter* (1995) 6–7.

———. "Women's Ordination and Infallibility: Waiting for Vatican III." *The Tablet* (1995) 1616–18.

LaCugna, Catherine Mowry. "Catholic Women as Ministers and Theologians." *America* (1992) 4–15.

———. *God for Us: The Trinity and Christian Life*. San Francisco: Harper, 1991.

LaCugna, Catherine Mowry, ed. *Freeing Theology: The Essentials of Theology in Feminist Perspective*. San Francisco: Harper, 1993.

LeGrand, Hervé-Marie. "The Indelible Character and the Theology of Ministry." *Concilium* 4 (1972) 54–62.

———. "La réalisation de l'eglise en un lieu." In *Initiation à la pratique de la théologie: Dogmatique III*, edited by Bernard Lauret and Francois Refoulé, 143–345. Paris: Cerf, 1983.

Lerner, Gerda. *The Creation of Feminist Consciousness: From the Middle Ages to 1870*. New York: Oxford University Press, 1993.

———. *The Creation of Patriarchy*. New York: Oxford University Press, 1986.

Little, Joyce A. Review of *The Church with a Human Face* by Edward Schillebeeckx. *The Thomist* 52 (1988) 158–65.

Luther, Martin. *Three Treatises*. Philadelphia: Muhlenberg, 1960.

McBrien, Richard. *Ministry: A Theological, Pastoral Handbook*. San Francisco: Harper & Row, 1987.

McCormack, Irene. "Do This in Memory of Me." *Compass Theology Review* 25 (1991) 33–35.

McGinniss, Michael J. Review of *The Church with a Human Face*, by Edward Schillebeeckx. *Horizons* 13 (1986) 432–33.

Messer, Donald E. *Contemporary Images of Christian Ministry*. Nashville, TN: Abingdon, 1989.

Metz, Johann-Baptist, and Jürgen Moltmann, eds. *Faith and the Future: Essays on Theology, Solidarity and Modernity*. New York: Orbis, 1995.

Michiels, Robrecht. Review of *Church: The Human Story of God*, by Edward Schillebeeckx. *Louvain Studies* 17 (1992) 65–68.

Miller, Joanne. Review of *The Church with a Human Face*, by Edward Schillebeeckx. *The Living Light* 23 (1986) 76–77.

National Catholic Reporter. "Women's Ordination Ban tied to Inferiority, Draft says." *National Catholic Reporter* 32 (1996) 6.

National Conference of Catholic Bishops. *The Sacramentary*. Collegeville, MN: Liturgical, 1974.

Neu, Diann. "Our Name is Church: The Experience of Catholic-Christian Feminist liturgies." *Concilium* 152 (1982) 75–84.

Neuger, Christie Cozad, ed. *The Arts of Ministry: Feminist-Womanist Approaches*. Louisville, KY: Westminster John Knox, 1996.

Neuner, J., and J. Dupuis. *The Christian Faith in the Doctrinal Documents of the Catholic Church*. London: Collins, 1983.

O'Brien, Kathleen, and Margaret Early. "Women: Leadership in Ministry." *Chicago Studies* 35 (1996) 156–76.

Obrist, Willy. "A Consecrated Hierarchy—an Obstacle to a Democratizating of the Catholic Church." *Concilium* 5 (1992) 27–37.

Ordination of Catholic Women. "A Gospel to be Proclaimed." Canberra: Ordination of Catholic Women, 1995.

———. "The Hour has Come." Kingston, ACT: Ordination of Catholic Women, 1997.

———. "Czech Woman Priest asserts the Validity of her Orders." *OCW News* 5.2 (1998) 6.

O'Meara, Thomas Franklin. *Theology of Ministry*. New Jersey: Paulist, 1983.

O'Neill, Mary Aquin. "Current Theology: The Nature of Women and the Method of Theology." *Theological Studies* 56 (1995) 730–42.

Ormerod, Neil. "Quarrels with the Method of Correlation." *Theological Studies* 57 (1996) 707–19.

———. "Towards a Systematic Theology of Ministry: A Catholic Perspective." *Pacifica* 8 (1995) 74–96.

Osborne, Kenan. *Ministry: Lay Ministry in the Roman Catholic Church*. New York: Paulist, 1993.

———. *Priesthood: A History of the Ordained Ministry in the Roman Catholic Church*. New York: Paulist, 1988.

Parker, Paul Plenge, ed. *Standing with the Poor: Theological Reflections on Economic Reality*. Cleveland, OH: Pilgrim, 1992.

Paul, Camille. "A Plethora of Phoebes." In *Faith and Culture: Challenges to Ministry*, edited by Neil Brown, 75–86. Sydney: Catholic Institute of Sydney, 1989.

Pilarczyk, Archbishop Daniel. "Defining the Priesthood." *Origins: CNS Documentary Service* 20.19. (1990) 299–300.

Pontificale Romanum. *De ordinatione diaconi, presbyteri et episcopi*. Vatican City: Typis Polyglottis Vaticanis, 1971.

Portier, William L. "Ministry from Above and/or Ministry from Below: An Examination of the Ecclesial Basis of Ministry according to Edward Schillebeeckx." *Communio* 12 (1985) 173–91.

Bibliography

Power, David N. *Gifts that Differ: Lay Ministries Established and Unestablished.* New York: Pueblo, 1980.

———. "Roman Catholic Theologies of Eucharistic Communion: A Contribution to Ecumenical Conversation." *Theological Studies* 57 (1996) 587–610.

———. "Sacrament: Event Eventing." In *A Promise of Presence: Studies in Honor of David N. Power,* edited by Michael Downey and Richard Fragomeni, 271–99. Washington, DC: Pastoral, 1992.

Primavesi, Anne, and Jennifer Henderson. *Our God Has No Favorites: A Liberation Theology of the Eucharist.* Tunbridge Wells, UK: Burns and Oates, 1989.

Procter-Smith, Marjorie. *In Her Own Rite: Constructing Feminist Liturgical Tradition.* Nashville, TN: Abingdon, 1990.

Purcell, Michael. "On the Ethical Nature of Priesthood." *The Heythrop Journal* 39.3 (1998) 298–314.

Rademacher, William J. *Lay Ministry: A Theological, Spiritual and Pastoral Handbook.* New York: Crossroad, 1996.

Rahner, Karl. *The Priesthood.* New York: Seabury, 1973.

———. *The Shape of the Church to Come.* New York: Seabury, 1974.

Rahner, Karl, et al., eds. *Sacramentum mundi: An Encyclopedia of Theology.* London: Burns and Oates, 1969.

Ranke-Heinemann, Uta. *Eunuchs for the Kingdom of Heaven: Women, Sexuality and the Catholic Church.* New York: Doubleday, 1990.

Ratzinger, Joseph. "Doctrinal Congregation on New Work by Father Schillebeeckx." *Origins: NC Documentary Service* 16 (1986) 344.

———. "Doctrinal Congregation Note on Response by Father Schillebeeckx." *Origins NC Documentary Service* 14 (1984) 526.

———. "The Minister of the Eucharist: Vatican Congregation's Letter to Bishops." *Origins: NC Documentary Service* 13 (1983) 229–33.

———. "Who can Preside at the Eucharist? Vatican Letter to Father Schillebeeckx." *Origins: NC Documentary Service* 14 (1985) 525.

Rausch, Thomas. *The Roots of the Catholic Tradition.* Wilmington: Glazier, 1986.

Rhodes, Lynn N. *Co-creating: A Feminist Vision of Ministry.* Philadelphia: Westminster, 1987.

Rice, David. *Shattered Vows: Exodus from the Priesthood.* London: Michael Joseph, 1990.

Richardson, Alan, ed. *A Dictionary of Christian Theology.* London: SCM, 1969.

Richardson, Alan, and John Bowden, eds. *A New Dictionary of Christian Theology.* London: SCM, 1983.

Roberts, Tom. "Dulles Urges Bishops to Enforce Papal No." *National Catholic Reporter* (1996) 6.

———. "Unanimous Voice is Recommended, but Bishops Divided on Women's Issue." *National Catholic Reporter* (1996) 7.

Ross, Susan A. *Extravagant Affections: A Feminist Sacramental Theology.* New York: Continuum, 1998.

———. "God's Embodiment and Women." In *Freeing Theology: The Essentials of Theology in Feminist Perspective,* edited by Catherine Mowry LaCugna, 185–209. San Francisco: HarperSanFrancisco, 1993.

Ruether, Rosemary Radford. *The Church Against Itself.* London: Sheed and Ward, 1967.

———. "Feminist Theology and Spirituality." In *Christian Feminism: Visions of a New Humanity,* edited by Judith L. Weidman, 9–32. San Francisco: Harper & Row, 1984.

———. "The Future of Feminist Theology in the Academy." *Journal of the American Academy of Religion* 53 (1985) 703–13.
———. *New Woman, New Earth*. New York: Seabury, 1974.
———. *Sexism and God-talk: Towards a Feminist Theology*. London: SCM, 1983.
———. *Women-Church: Theology and Practice*. San Francisco, Harper & Row, 1988.
Ruether, Rosemary Radford, ed. *Religion and Sexism: Images of Women in the Jewish and Christian Traditions*. New York: Simon and Schuster, 1974.
Ruether, Rosemary Radford, and Eleanor McLaughlin. *Women of Spirit: Female Leadership in the Jewish and Christian Traditions*. New York: Simon and Schuster, 1979.
Russell, Letty M. "Authority and the Challenge of Feminist Interpretation". In *Feminist Interpretation of the Bible*, edited by Letty M. Russell, 137–46. Philadelphia: Westminster, 1985.
———. *Church in the Round: Feminist Interpretations of the Church*. Louisville, KY: Westminster/John Knox, 1993.
———. *Household of Freedom: Authority in Feminist Theology*. Philadelphia: Westminster, 1987.
———. *Human Liberation in a Feminist Perspective: A Theology*. Philadelphia: Westminster, 1974.
———. "Women and Ministry." In *Sexist Religion and Women in the Church: No More Silence!* edited by Alice L. Hageman, 47–62. New York: Association, 1974.
———. "Women and Ministry: Problem or Possibility?" In *Christian Feminism: Visions of a New Humanity*, edited by Judith L. Weidman, 75–92. San Francisco: Harper & Row, 1984.
Russell, Letty M., ed. *Feminist Interpretation of the Bible*. Philadelphia: Westminster, 1985.
Sacred Congregation for the Clergy. *Inter Insigniores: Declaration on the Question of the Admission of Women to the Ministerial Priesthood*. Washington, DC: United States Catholic Conference Publications Office, 1977.
Schaefer, Mary, and Sara Butler. "Forum: Ordaining Women." *Worship* 63 (1989) 467–71.
Sheets, John R. "Forum: the Ordination of Women." *Worship* 65 (1991) 451–61.
Schillebeeckx, Edward. *Christ: The Christian Experience in the Modern World*. London: SCM, 1980.
———. "The Christian Community and its Office Bearers." *Concilium* 133 (1980) 95–133.
———. *Church: The Human Story of God*. London: SCM, 1990.
———. *The Church with a Human Face: A New and Expanded Theology of Ministry*. New York: Crossroad, 1992.
———. *For the Sake of the Gospel*. London: SCM, 1989.
———. *God Among Us: The Gospel Proclaimed*. New York: Crossroad, 1983.
———. *God is New Each Moment*. Edinburgh: T & T Clark, 1983.
———. *I am a Happy Theologian*. London: SCM, 1994.
———. "In Memoriam Marie-Dominique Chenu (1895–1990)." *New Theology Review* 3 (1990) 89–91.
———. *Interim Report on the Books, Jesus and Christ*. London: SCM, 1980.
———. *Jesus: An Experiment in Christology*. London: William Collins, 1979.
———. *The Language of Faith: Essays on Jesus, Theology and the Church*. New York: Orbis, 1995.
———. *Ministry: Leadership in the Community of Jesus Christ*. New York: Crossroad, 1980.
———. *The Mission of the Church*. New York: Seabury, 1973.

Bibliography

———. *The Understanding of Faith: Interpretation and Criticism.* New York: Seabury, 1974.

———. *World and Church.* London: Sheed and Ward, 1971.

Schmidt, Richard. "Phenomenology." In *The Encyclopedia of Philosophy: Vol. 5 and 6,* edited by Paul Edwards, 135–51. New York: Macmillan and Free, 1967:

Schneiders, Sandra M. "The Bible and Feminism." In *Freeing Theology: The Essentials of Theology in Feminist Perspective,* edited by Catherine Mowry LaCugna, 185–209. San Francisco: HarperSanFrancisco, 1993.

Schoof, Mark. *Breakthrough: Beginnings of the New Catholic Theology.* Dublin: Gill and Macmillan, 1970.

———. "E. Schillebeeckx: Twenty-five years in Nijmegen." *Theology Digest* 37.4 (1990) 313–32.

———. "Masters in Israel: VII. The Later Theology of Edward Schillebeeckx." *Clergy Review* 55 (1970) 943–60.

Schoof, Mark, ed. *The Schillebeeckx Case: Official Exchange of Letters and Documents in the Investigation of Fr. Edward Schillebeeckx by the Sacred Congregation for the Doctrine of the Faith, 1976-1980.* New York: Paulist, 1984.

Schreiter, Robert J., ed. Review of *Eglise et ministères: pour un dialogue critique avec Edward Schillebeeckx,* by Pierre Grelot. *Theological Studies* 45 (1984) 204–5.

———. Review of *Ministry: Leadership in the Community of Jesus Christ,* by Edward Schillebeeckx. *Theological Studies* 42 (1981) 678–80.

———. *The Schillebeeckx Reader.* New York: Crossroad, 1984.

———. "Taking Christian Experience Seriously: A Profile of Edward Schillebeeckx." *The Critic* 42 (1998) 9–21.

Schreiter, Robert J., and Mary Catherine Hilkert, eds. *The Praxis of Christian Experience: An Introduction to the Theology of Edward Schillebeeckx.* San Francisco: Harper & Row, 1989.

Seasoltz, Kevin. "Contemporary Eucharistic Celebrations: Mixed Motives and Meanings." *Concilium* 152 (1982) 33–40.

Seper, Cardinal Franjo. *Declaration on the Question of the Admission of Women to the Ministerial Priesthood.* Washington, DC: US Catholic Conference Office, 1976.

Stacpole, Alberic. Review of *The Church with a Human Face,* by Edward Schillebeeckx. *The Month* 19 (1986) 103–4.

———. "Revolution in the Concept of Priesthood." *The Month* 15 (1982) 330–35.

Stevenson, J., ed. *Creeds, Councils and Controversies.* London: SPCK, 1966.

Sullivan, Francis, A. Review of *The Church with a Human Face,* by Edward Schillebeeckx. *The Tablet* 240 (1986) 11–12.

The Sunday Missal: A New Edition. London: Collins, 1982.

Swidler, Leonard, ed. *Consensus in Theology: A Dialogue with Hans Küng and Edward Schillebeeckx.* Philadelphia: Westminster, 1980.

Swidler, Leonard, and Swidler, Arlene, eds. *Women Priests: A Catholic Commentary on the Vatican Declaration.* New York: Paulist, 1977.

Thérèse of Lisieux. *Autobiography of a Saint: The Story of a Soul.* Translated by Ronald Knox. Glasgow: Fount, 1977.

Tillich, Paul. *Systematic Theology, Vol. 1.* Chicago: University of Chicago Press, 1963.

Tolhurst, James. Review of *Church: The Human Story of God,* by Edward Schillebeeckx. *Priest and People* 5 (1991) 81–82.

Torjesen, Karen Jo. *When Women were Priests: Women's Leadership in the Early Church and the Scandal of their Subordination in the Rise of Christianity.* San Francisco: Harper, 1995.
Torrance, T.F. *Royal Priesthood: A Theology of Ordained Ministry.* Edinburgh: T & T Clark, 1993.
Tracy, David. *The Analogical Imagination.* London: SCM, 1981.
———. *Blessed Rage for Order: The New Pluralism in Theology.* New York: Seabury, 1975.
———. "Hermeneutical Reflections in the New Paradigm." In *Paradigm Change in Theology,* edited by Hans Küng and David Tracy, 34–62. New York: Crossroad, 1991.
———. "The Uneasy Alliance Reconceived: Catholic Theological Method, Modernity and Postmodernity." *Theological Studies* 50 (1989) 548–70.
Ulloa, Margaret. "Extending Ordained Ministry." *The Way* (1995) 3–12.
Untener, Kenneth. "Forum: The Ordination of Women: Can the Horizons Widen?" *Worship* 65 (1991) 50–59.
van der Meer, Haye. *Women Priests in the Catholic Church? A Theological-historical Investigation.* Philadelphia: Temple University Press, 1973.
van der Pleog, J.P.M. "E. Schillebeeckx and the Catholic Priesthood." *Homiletic and Pastoral Review* 82 (1982) 22–48.
Van Merrienboer, Edward. "Christian Ministry in Light of Schillebeeckx's Theology of Grace." *Spirituality Today* 34 (1982) 144–54.
Vanhoye, Albert and Henri Crouzel. "The Ministry in the Church: Reflections on a Recent Publication." *Clergy Review* 68 (1983) 155–68.
Verdesi, Elizabeth Howell. *In But Still Out: Women in the Church.* Philadelphia: Westminster, 1976.
Vlk, Miroslav. "Cardinal Confirms Catholic Woman's Secret Ordination." *The Tablet* (1996) 768.
Volf, Miroslav. *After Our Likeness: The Church as the Image of the Trinity.* Grand Rapids, MI: Eerdmans, 1998.
Von Balthasar, Hans Urs. "Retrieving the Tradition: How Weighty is the Argument from "Uninterrupted Tradition" to Justify the Male Priesthood?" *Communio* 23 (1996) 185–98.
Watkins, Clare. "Ministry, Muddle and Mystery: Reflections on Ordination and Service from a Lay Perspective." *The Way Supplement* 83 (1995) 80–89.
Weaver, Mary Jo. *New Catholic Women: A Contemporary Challenge to Traditional Religious Authority.* San Francisco: Harper & Row, 1985.
Welch, Sharon D. *A Feminist Ethic of Risk.* Minneapolis: Fortress, 1990.
Whitehead, James, D., and Evelyn Eaton Whitehead. *The Promise of Partnership: Leadership and Ministry in an Adult Church.* San Francisco: Harper, 1991.
Wilson-Kastner, Patricia. *Faith, Feminism and the Christ.* Philadelphia: Fortress, 1983.
Wind, James P., et al., eds. *Clergy Ethics in a Changing Society: Mapping the Terrain.* Philadelphia: Westminster/John Knox, 1991.
Winter, Miriam Therese, et al. *Defecting in Place: Women Claiming Responsibility for Their Own Lives.* New York: Crossroad, 1995.
Wister, Robert, ed. *Priests: Identity and Ministry.* Wilmington, DE: Michael Glazier, 1990.
Wood, Susan. "Ecclesial Koinonia in Ecumenical Dialogues." *One in Christ* 30.2 (1994) 124–45.
———. "Priestly Identity: Sacrament to the Ecclesial Community." *Worship* 69 (1995) 109–27.
Zizioulas, John D. *Being as Communion: Studies in Personhood and the Church.* London: Darton, Longman & Todd, 1985.

www.ingramcontent.com/pod-product-compliance
Lightning Source LLC
Chambersburg PA
CBHW070051200426
43193CB00054B/1381